Inna Turch

Welcome Ho

Inna Turchyn

Welcome Home
The Path Back to Me

How to Find Inner Peace and Achieve Happiness

A Guided Self-Discovery, Gratitude and Manifestation Journal

Explained with 33 stories from the author's life

Translated from the German
by Heather Whitehall-Trochon

Disclaimer: This book is meant as a source of valuable information for the reader, however it is not meant as a substitute for direct expert assistance. If such level of assistance is required, the services of a competent medical or mental health professional should be sought.

Copyright © 2014, 2025 by Inna Turchyn

Published by Stanislav Turchyn

All rights reserved. No portion of this book may be reproduced, stored in a retrieval system, or transmitted, in any form, or by any means, electronic, mechanical, photocopying, recording, or otherwise, without written permission from the publisher or author, except by reviewer who may quote brief passages in a review. For information about this title, please contact: Stanislav Turchyn, Viktoriastr. 22, 65189 Wiesbaden, Germany, E-mail: stanislav.turchyn@gmail.com.

Translated from the German by Heather Whitehall-Trochon
Cover design und photography by Stanislav Turchyn

Bibliographic information from the German National Library:
The German National Library documents this publication in the German National Bibliography; detailed bibliographic data is available on the Internet under: http://dnb.dnb.de.

ISBN: 979-8-31-070780-1

2nd edition 2025

Every man is the architect of his own fortune
—Appius Claudius Caecus

CONTENTS

ACKNOWLEDGEMENTS IX
INTRODUCTION 1
   My happiness is my responsibility 1
   How this book can help you 2
   What you will find in this book 3
PART I: JOURNEY OF SELF-DISCOVERY 5
CHAPTER 1: STORIES AND LESSONS LEARNT 7
   Story 1: Searching or finding…? 7
   Story 2: A healthy "don't care" attitude 10
   Story 3: When dreams come true 13
   Story 4: Can we all win…? Of course! 16
   Story 5: Share your smiles 19
   Story 6: Never say never! 22
   Story 7: God moves in mysterious ways 25
   Story 8: I don't know what I want – I don't want what I know ... 28
   Story 9: It makes me afraid…? Try it! 31
   Story 10: Making things worse for the better 34
   Story 11: When you try to please everybody 37
   Story 12: What is good and what is bad? 40
   Story 13: Take advantage of opportunities! 43
   Story 14: Listen to your intuition! 46
   Story 15: It's better to die and to be left in peace 49
   Story 16: Fortune smiles on the brave! 52
   Story 17: And just where is the happy medium…? 55
   Story 18: Endlessly positive! 58
   Story 19: Coincidences are never a coincidence 61
   Story 20: Love can move mountains! 64
   Story 21: And then along came happiness 67
   Story 22: The buck stops here! 70
   Story 23: Over and over again 72
   Story 24: Allow yourself to be inspired! 75
   Story 25: The finger points at the moon 77
   Story 26: Boomerang 80
   Story 27: My decision – my responsibility! 83

Story 28: Majority.. 86
Story 29: 'Why?' Is that a question or a wish?........................ 89
Story 30: Bless you!.. 91
Story 31: A conversation with the shadows 94
Story 32: Are you in harmony with yourself...?..................... 97
Story 33: Peace and comfort!... 100

CHAPTER 2: FROM GRATITUDE TO MANIFESTATION 103
Light at the end of the tunnel 103
A brief report 10 years later 105

PART II: ROADMAP TO HAPPINESS **111**

CHAPTER 3: INTRODUCTION TO THE ROADMAP 113

CHAPTER 4: A STEP-BY-STEP GUIDE 117
Step 1: Analysis of the current situation............................... 117
Step 2: Creation of a vision for a happy life 122
Step 3: Taking action.. 128

CHAPTER 5: BASIC PRACTICES 133
Working with problems 133
Working with affirmations 137
Working with feelings and emotions.................................... 139
Working with dreams 141

CHAPTER 6: YOUR GRATITUDE AND MANIFESTATION JOURNAL
.... 145
What am I grateful for in life? 145
What do I wish for in life? 148
My happy life 151
Affirm your happy life 159
Visualise your happy life... 159
Enjoy your day 159
Report on your progress.. 160

ABOUT THE AUTHOR 171

ACKNOWLEDGEMENTS

First and foremost, I offer my heartfelt gratitude to the divine power, which is inherent in each of us, for the idea for this book and for the support in its realisation.

Since the second edition of this book was only possible thanks to the first edition, I would first like to wholeheartedly thank everyone who helped and supported me in the preparation of the latter.

My special thanks for the collaboration on the second edition go to my husband Stanislav Turchyn. His help in structuring and describing the approach and in creating clear diagrams was invaluable.

I am also very grateful to my son Alexander Turchyn for his contribution to this book. His ideas and feedback were a valuable addition that helped to make the description of the approach more reader-friendly.

I would like to express my sincere gratitude to my colleague Svetlana Rudakova-Safir, systemic family therapist (German Society for Systemic Therapy and Family Therapy or "DGSF"), for her kind support and invaluable ideas. Her professional opinion helped me to improve the description of the approach and make it more accessible.

I would also like to say a heartfelt thank you to Olena Harashchenko, Iryna Lobova, Inna Petrova and Iryna Trofymova for their questions, ideas and comments that helped to facilitate the practicality of the approach.

I would especially like to thank Heather Whitehall-Trochon for the wonderful translation of both editions into English.

INTRODUCTION

My happiness is my responsibility

We are all born to be happy. This is my belief.

Attracting only what you really want into your life is both an art and a daily task. Otherwise, you waste your life's energy chasing after one thought or another. In the end, we do not know what we have achieved. And then what becomes of those heartfelt desires? Who then gives them their attention and love...?

It seems we should be taught this from an early age. After all, the greater the number of happy people there are on our planet, the better the world around us would be.

Some may have been lucky in life and learnt it from their parents or someone close to them. In my life, unfortunately, there was neither a "happy mum" nor a "happy dad" from whom I could learn how to live a happy life. Of course, there were moments of joy in my parents' lives, as there were in mine: love, the birth of a child, etc., but I generally had to learn everything from my own experience and get my own bruises. Some experiences were so painful that it's a miracle I survived them.

The story of how this book came about began in Christmas 2011, when I learnt from my doctor that I had been diagnosed with hepatitis C. Shortly before that, I found myself in a situation from which I saw no way out, leading to a strong fear of the future that I couldn't overcome.

Three years ago, thanks to social media, I got back in touch with a man I had been in love with since I was a teenager. We had broken up many years ago but he would pop up in my dreams from time to time, which caused me a lot of pain. Shortly before I was diagnosed with hepatitis C, he asked me if there was a place for him in my life. This question caught me completely by surprise and I was terrified.

Whatever future scenario I imagined, none of them made me feel good. I went through different options to try and figure out where I could go, but I only sank deeper into negativity. To distract myself from my troubling thoughts, I started listening to pleasant music, meditating and doing things that made me happy. But that didn't help and I became ill.

During my therapy, when I was on the brink of death, I began to analyse various situations from my life. In doing so, I drew upon my knowledge and professional experience in psychology and systemic therapy, among other things. I began to regularly put the lessons I learnt from each situation into practice and overcome my fears.

Thanks to this analysis, I was able to formulate goals that served as a light at the end of the tunnel and inspired me to keep going. I also became convinced that it was possible to achieve these goals.

When I had finished my analysis, my doctor told me that I was healthy again. Wanting to share my experiences, I published the first edition of this book a few months later.

How this book can help you

More than ten years have now passed. During this time, I put what I had learnt into practice.

This has helped me to:

- overcome fears and anxiety
- find inner peace and gain confidence
- develop healthy self-love
- start to appreciate all the things that bring me joy in life
- improve my health
- overcome seemingly insurmountable problems
- formulate wishes and goals, even if I didn't know exactly what I wanted
- manifest what I desired
- achieve goals, even in uncertain circumstances
- reduce the number of negative feelings and thoughts and to harness negative emotions for my own benefit
- better understand and utilise my dreams
- liberate myself from recurring painful dreams

The desire to pass on my accumulated experience prompted me to expand the book by describing the practices I use. Journaling exercises invite you to start your own journey of self-discovery. The Gratitude and Manifestation Journal gives you the opportunity to put the "Roadmap to Happiness" into practice in your specific case.

What you will find in this book

In the first part of the book, "Journey of Self-Discovery", I analyse 33 different situations from my own life, which deal with what I wanted, the path taken to reach my goal, what I achieved in the end, whether I was ultimately satisfied with the result and why. It's about both success stories and failures, as well as what I learnt along the way.

These stories give you the opportunity to think about whether something similar has happened in your own life, to write your own stories and to ask yourself the same questions I asked myself.

All situations described here are in the order in which they ran through my mind. As I wrote the final story, not only did I have clarity on what it is that I want, but also how I will proceed with all of this in the future.

Finally, I describe the goals I set myself in the first edition and briefly report on the extent to which I managed to realise these goals over time.

The second part, "Roadmap to Happiness", which I wrote together with my husband Stanislav Turchyn, who, like me, used all the practices described in the book during those ten years, outlines my approach to building a happy life.

The roadmap is written in the form of a practical step-by-step guide with exercises and illustrated with examples from my life, which are analysed in the first part of the book. It consists of three steps, four basic practices for working with problems, affirmations, feelings and emotions, as well as dreams, and a gratitude and manifestation journal.

Focusing on your own resources, goal orientation and positive thinking are an essential part of this approach, which uses elements from various areas of psychology, neuro-linguistic programming (NLP), as well as working with mental training techniques.

My aim is for my book to inspire you and help you to find inner peace and build a happy life. I hope you enjoy reading it and wish you success on your path to happiness.

I would be very grateful if you would share your feedback on the book as a review on Amazon.

PART I:
Journey of Self-Discovery

CHAPTER 1:

STORIES AND LESSONS LEARNT

Story 1:
Searching or finding...?

During a complementary course of studies, in which I participated, there was a student in our group who was a psychologist by profession. She made us an extremely interesting proposal. We should compile career plans and give them to her for evaluation. To this end she distributed special forms, which we completed.

Well, what did I learn from the one-to-one counselling session? I was made aware of the fact that I had entered "looking for work" in the line "goal". I didn't immediately understand where the problem could lie. I was studying and simultaneously looking for a job. After all, that is the best way to find one. It's logical, isn't it?

I was thrown into a turmoil by her question, as to whether I wished to eternally be in search of a position, or whether I in fact wished to find a place of work.

'What am I searching for then? Of course, to find one!' I said, and then it became clear to me that I really had a strange goal.

I gave some thought as to how my search for work had progressed with such a goal... It was as though the scales fell from my eyes. I had found – and applied for – interesting job offers. I had often been invited to job interviews, but they didn't lead to anything. This had repeated itself over and over again. These were the best prerequisites for an eternal search for work, weren't they?

'In all likelihood, it is actually important that the goal isn't viewed as a process, but rather as a clearly defined final state...,' I thought and replaced "looking for work" with "finding work", and I didn't just do so on paper – but also in my mind.

And, guess what? The situation suddenly changed. Barely had a month passed since the end of my studies and I had already conducted seminars of my own.

My thoughts, comments and conclusions

When I wish to search for something, I will not find it until I have another wish. Therefore, before wishing for something, it is important to remind ourselves of what the desired goal should be: a process or the final state…? Do I want to search or to find, to do something or finish something, to learn or master something, to wait or to have meetings…? These are entirely my own decisions!

Your story

Describe a situation from your life that comes to mind in relation to the story you have just read.

Story 2:
A healthy "don't care" attitude

During my complementary studies, two fellow students and I had the opportunity to receive a scholarship for further training.

It was such a great surprise and I felt very excited. I prepared all of the necessary papers and sent them to the institution that had selected the scholarship students. I received a very impersonal rejection letter in which it stated that my qualifications didn't meet with their requirements. This naturally put me in a sad mood. But what could I do in this situation?

'If it's not to be, then it's not to be. End of story,' I told myself. I wrote an e-mail to the university concerning my rejection, and found my peace of mind once more.

How was I to know that my tutor didn't want to accept the rejection just like that? He began to negotiate with the institute in question. I was supposed to then send additional documents, which I did.

However, my inner state had already changed. I was absolutely calm and equally as prepared to receive an "acceptance" as I was a "rejection". I could barely believe it when an exception was made for me and I received the scholarship!

My thoughts, comments and conclusions

When I want something so badly that it hurts, then it escapes me. When I am satisfied with all that I have, but it would intrinsically be nice if a certain wish were fulfilled, then opportunities arise for it to be realised. Whether I seize the opportunities or not is another matter. However, whether I receive these opportunities or not is dependent upon how I feel (am I suffering or am I in the frame of mind: "It is super if I get it, if not – then that's fine too").

Thus, a healthy "don't care" attitude is a good thing, but it is not always possible to remain in this state... Although, it is already very helpful when you understand what you feel and in which direction you are heading.

Your story

Describe a situation from your life that comes to mind in relation to the story you have just read.

Story 3:
When dreams come true...

I once had the desire to support unemployed people in their search for work. After a short period of time, I obtained a position that perfectly corresponded with my wish. There was a great deal of work. I rolled my sleeves up and began my duties with utter enthusiasm. However, things weren't what they had first seemed...

Upon closer inspection I realised that not all project participants wanted to find a job. And the collaboration with some of my colleagues didn't exactly run smoothly.

I then asked myself whether I had imagined my work to be like this? Or was I so much concentrated on my task that I had lost sight of certain aspects of it...?

And that's precisely what had happened! Where was the fun in the work? Nice colleagues? Motivated participants? It was only once I was immersed in the work that I began to think about it. Therefore, I ultimately received what I had ordered. Nothing else had appeared on the "shopping list".

My thoughts, comments and conclusions

That's precisely how it happens in my life. Although the wishes are fulfilled, they are fulfilled literally. If I want to try something out – like working with unemployed people, for example –, then I'm welcome to do so! Whether I will enjoy it is quite another matter...

So, what do I really want – certain events, things, acquaintances or positive feelings, and namely that these feelings are reflected in all aspects of my wish that are of interest to me...? If this concerns a place of work, then it should be one in which I like everything about it. Otherwise, it may be that a single unsatisfactory aspect will cast a shadow on all of the others.

Over the course of time, it may be that there is also something that we dislike about a new place of work. However, we develop further and our wishes change. And when that happens, it is then the moment to ask ourselves a few questions: 'What do I desire now? Is it possible to realise my wish without a change of job, or is a new position the better option after all?'

Your story

Describe a situation from your life that comes to mind in relation to the story you have just read.

Story 4:
Can we all win...? Of course!

For quite a long time I worked in a great team and enjoyed doing so. I grew so accustomed to it that I took this comfort for granted. And it was precisely at this moment that I got a new colleague. To begin with I didn't immediately understand what bothered me, since – viewed from the outside – everything looked rosy.

Later I noticed that I began to feel uneasy at the mere thought of my colleague. 'Things cannot carry on like this!' I thought and tried to determine exactly what it was that disturbed me. It was as though she saw me as a rival, rather than a partner. All in all, I felt uncomfortable.

'If I don't like this situation, what is it that would make me happy?' I asked myself. In the process, I only had one single thought that made me feel comfortable. It concerned the collaboration with people, with whom I find working to be easy and pleasant.

I therefore decided that, every time I found myself thinking of her, I would consciously and immediately replace this thought with one about a fantastic working environment. In so doing, I thought about my former colleague – with whom the working atmosphere was very pleasant – and I held this thought for as long as possible. I thereby didn't wish anything towards my colleague at all and concentrated exclusively on myself.

At the same time, I undertook other steps that made our collaboration easier. Among other things, I reduced our contact to a minimum.

Barely two weeks had gone by when my colleague delightedly announced to me that she had found a new, very interesting job, and that I was to get a new colleague... And working together with him was an absolute dream!

My thoughts, comments and conclusions

There are a couple of aspects that I find interesting in this situation...

As long as I wish for a good team or something else, then that's what I will have. If I stop thinking about this, then it's my own fault. A comparison can be drawn with shopping. If I forget to go shopping before the shops close, then I'll go hungry. So, if something pleases me, it makes sense to continue to wish it for myself.

Something else occurred to me. Instead of wasting the power of thought on an unpleasant individual or situation, it is better to concentrate on your personal goal, without wishing something negative to the other person in the process. As a consequence, everybody is a winner!

Your story

Describe a situation from your life that comes to mind in relation to the story you have just read.

Story 5:
Share your smiles

For a while, as part of the road safety campaign, motorways featured posters along the lines of "foot off the accelerator", which looked as follows: tragic images of victims in a black frame, black crosses, sad children, wives, parents etc. Very life-affirming! Don't you agree?

It was quite eerie when I was travelling, and tragic images and black crosses continually appeared before my eyes. As a result, the emotions I felt were far from positive. And this was whilst I was driving! My acquaintances, with whom I discussed this, didn't like these posters either. Although they intrinsically found the idea, that drivers should drive more carefully, to be very good. But the interpretation... People indeed prefer to experience a positive emotion!

And, to this end, my husband and I gave some thought as to how the posters could look so that they would appeal to us. We subsequently came up with several creative ideas.

We then sought out both the client as well as the designer of the posters and sent them e-mails in which we presented our ideas, along with a couple of examples as to how they could look in order to be enlightening and to awaken positive emotions. At the same time, we wrote about what we liked about the campaign, what we didn't and why not.

And guess what...? After a period of time, new posters appeared. Not only did these put us in a good mood, but they had the same impact on other people too.

My thoughts, comments and conclusions

So, what's the point of all of that...? If I wish to improve something in my private life, my town or my country, then it makes more sense not to wait until someone else does it for me. Otherwise, you can wait forever!

Has the time come to ask yourself: 'What can I do in this situation?' And if you have a good idea, then get started! After all, when you do a good deed for yourself, then you are ultimately also doing this for others too.

Your story

Describe a situation from your life that comes to mind in relation to the story you have just read.

Story 6:
Never say never!

When I chose my first foreign language at school, I said that I would never in my life learn German. I found the language to be coarse and tuneless. It is for this reason that I selected English. Well, indeed, for many years I was far removed from German... but one day we decided to emigrate to Germany.

And how could things now progress without German? Not at all! I therefore began to learn it and I did so with determination. To my amazement, the more I learnt the language, the more fun I had with it. I discovered that German is not at all coarse sounding, but rather quite the opposite – it is very melodious indeed.

And now I am living in this country, I work as a trainer and a coach and I teach German! At the same time, I am enjoying the language that I never wanted to learn.

My thoughts, comments and conclusions

If I claim that I will never do something, then I can assume it is this very thing that will occur – even in its most extreme form. In my case, I was simply lucky.

Therefore, before saying "never" or "under no circumstances", you should think carefully about whether you are prepared to receive the full extent of that which you have rejected.

Your story

Describe a situation from your life that comes to mind in relation to the story you have just read.

Story 7:
God moves in mysterious ways

Shortly after emigrating to Germany, I participated – in my capacity as the beneficiary of a scholarship – in a programme for foreign academics, in order to complete an occupational internship.

Within the framework of the programme there were a series of seminars. One of them was job application training. It was during this very seminar that I got the idea that I would also very much like to conduct such training seminars for this foundation.

However, I couldn't imagine how I would be able to achieve this goal. In addition, we only had native instructors. I, on the other hand, was a foreigner, who didn't have a particularly good grasp of the German language.

Nevertheless, this subject was so interesting for me that I initially began to conduct such seminars in Russian for Russian-speaking immigrants. Seminars in German then came along as well.

After two years, during a complementary study course, I became acquainted with a woman from my group. She not only wanted to offer a training seminar on the same subject, but also for the same foundation. Can you imagine? 'There are coincidences in life, after all!' I told myself.

Only upon taking a closer look did it become clear to me that our ideas complemented each other very well. We developed the seminar concept together and presented it to the foundation. I now had a colleague!

A head of department at the foundation found our concept to be interesting and asked whether we were fundamentally prepared to integrate our idea in her training.

'Such a great combination!' I thought. Since this offer appealed to us, we accepted – after giving it some brief consideration.

Following the complementary course of study, I continued to conduct the seminars, but they were now in German. After approx. 6 months, it was suggested that my colleague and I conduct our first training seminar together.

Two and a half years ago, I took part in one such training seminar. I am now conducting the training, and indeed in such a fantastic team, that I could never have imagined possible.

My thoughts, comments and conclusions

There are goals in which the path to reach them is clear and distinct. For example, when I wanted to be an engineer, I knew that I must complete a course of studies. However, there are goals to which there is no predefined path.

Nevertheless, if I really want something, then I somehow make a few steps in the given direction. Since I wanted to conduct seminars for a certain foundation, I began to conduct this seminar for other organisations. I then met my future partner, which resulted in the idea of a joint training seminar, and in this way an offer appeared from the foundation with which I very much wanted to work.

I also did everything within my power in order to approach my goal, one step at a time. What would I have achieved if I had merely waited…?

In other words, whilst concentrating on my wish, I had also seen the possibilities to take a further step towards my goal. But I would never have been able to plan such a path!

Your story

Describe a situation from your life that comes to mind in relation to the story you have just read.

Story 8:
I don't know what I want –
I don't want what I know...

And that's exactly how it was. I didn't particularly like what I had undertaken for a career. And I didn't have a clue about what I wanted to do in the future. 'And what now?' I asked myself.

Sitting at home wasn't a solution either, since it was too boring for me not to have something to do. It is for this reason that I gave some thought about my desired place of work and wrote down everything that came to mind. In the process, I arrived at the following:

I would very much like to enjoy what I do (unfortunately it wasn't more detailed than that), how I do it and with whom I work. My clients, colleagues, employers and I are very satisfied with my work. I only need 10 minutes to walk to work from my home. I live in the centre of a town that inspires me.

However, I forgot to enter my salary expectations on this list. You can probably imagine the moment at which I gave some consideration to my salary!

Shortly afterwards my husband decided to find a new job. Thank goodness, in contrast to me, he knew what he wanted to do. He received several interesting offers and decided upon one of them. We moved to a very attractive town, in the centre of which we found an apartment.

'And where will I find a job, when I have no idea what I want to do?' I thought and decided to apply to diverse companies that work with immigrants. In so doing, I proposed everything that I could offer.

One day, in the newspaper, I saw the publicity for a company that was involved with foreigners. I applied to them and very soon received an invitation for an interview.

The manager of the company wanted to know how I had found the company, since no advertisement had been published. And I was taken aback by what he offered me. In my opinion, I wasn't qualified for the post – as I also told him on the spot. It concerned a literacy course for foreigners.

'Don't panic,' he said, 'I have the impression that this job is exactly the right one for you. And if you also find it interesting, then we'll talk about a licence and further training.'

'But I have never done it before! How should I manage to do it?' I asked. He recommended that I sit in on a course. At the same time, I could conduct part of the lesson. In the event that I decide for the job, we would then talk about the work once more.

Can you imagine it? After two weeks I was already giving lessons. And everything that I had wished for had been fulfilled. Of course, I also had a salary – but the pay in the social sector isn't very much.

My thoughts, comments and conclusions

I have no idea what you think, but the fact is: If I don't know exactly what I want, but I do know what I want to feel, then, strangely enough, I find that too.

Your story

Describe a situation from your life that comes to mind in relation to the story you have just read.

....

....

....

....

....

....

....

....

....

....

....

Story 9:
It makes me afraid...? Try it!

Several of my school teachers told me my calling was to be a teacher. But I wasn't sure about it. Although I used to dance and feel absolutely confident on the stage, I was nevertheless extremely afraid of speaking in public. For this reason, I never considered undertaking a teacher training course.

Instead, I studied at a technical university. Even giving talks in front of my group was a major challenge for me. When it was time for my thesis presentation, which would be made in front of many people, I panicked. My anxiety was especially great when I visualised myself in that situation. In order to calm down, I had to think about what could help me. Several ideas came to mind.

So, what did I do? After preparing the presentation, I invited my neighbour and presented my thesis in front of her. I wanted to hear her suggestions as to how I could improve it. She visited me on three occasions to observe the latest, improved version. Despite preparing my thesis very well and being able to present it, I still took a tranquiliser before making my speech!

After finishing my studies, I received two offers from the college for me to continue to study for a doctorate, which also meant teaching in a specific subject. It is for this reason that I turned the offers down.

I no longer know how it came about, but I gradually began to work in the social sector. However, my anxiety remained. At one point I saw an offer that concerned further training to be a lecturer in adult education. In order to feel more at ease, I participated in this further training.

I then began to conduct seminars. I was not completely free from anxiety to begin with, but I already felt better than before. Different methods and thorough preparation helped me a great deal with this. And, through the experience, I began to enjoy the work more.

My thoughts, comments and conclusions

I drew the following conclusions from this: If you are afraid to do something, it is helpful to do precisely that. Anxiety then no longer has a chance to take hold. And, indeed, the sooner you begin and the more often you do it, the better.

Your story

Describe a situation from your life that comes to mind in relation to the story you have just read.

Story 10:
Making things worse for the better

We once had a neighbour, who lived directly one floor below our apartment. Shortly after we moved in, she asked us if we could be quieter. Although we adhered to all of the house rules, I wanted to help her and spoke with my husband about what we could do in this respect.

After the steps undertaken by us (felt soundproofing pads, new slippers etc.), to our surprise she said we had become even louder. And what had been the point in doing all of this? And whom had it helped? Our neighbour? No. Us? Also no. As a consequence, I no longer had the desire to do something for her.

We then gave some thought as to what we actually wanted. This was comfort in the apartment and good relationships with the neighbours. But how could this be achieved...? Especially when the neighbour's hostility had become even greater. And the housing association was unable to help us.

We subsequently began to search for a new apartment, but were unable to find anything suitable. How was it then possible to find peace...?

I decided to behave like my husband and stopped thinking about our neighbour. In order to find peace, I concentrated on my wishes and ignored her – irrespective of what she did – as though she didn't exist.

To begin with, the situation only got worse. The neighbour was so angry and, day and night, shouted so loudly that none of the inhabitants in our building were able to find peace. I then heard that, through collecting signatures, the residents of a building were able to improve the situation with a neighbour, who was an alcoholic.

Previously, I would have simply ignored this case. This time it gave me an idea. I proposed that our housing association make a survey among all inhabitants of our building. We then received the news that our neighbour was moving out. This was truly wonderful news!

My thoughts, comments and conclusions

Once again, I wanted to do someone a favour – although I made my own life difficult in the process. In the end I was again dissatisfied and the relationship had broken down.

Therefore, if the thought of doing someone a favour, or something similar, awakens positive feelings in me, then it makes sense to act accordingly. However, if this isn't the case, then it should be considered carefully. For it always amounts to the same thing in the end: namely, to your disadvantage.

Perhaps it is better to concentrate my thoughts on my own wellbeing? If I don't, then who will...?

Your story

Describe a situation from your life that comes to mind in relation to the story you have just read.

Story 11:
When you try to please everybody

I once worked in a team in which I felt like a complete outsider. The thought that I didn't fit to the team stirred unpleasant feelings within me. So, I decided to stick to the rules of the team. At the time I wasn't thrilled by this idea, but I didn't have a better one.

I thought this sense of unease would pass with time, and that I would feel good. But this wasn't the case. I only felt worse. We were simply too different. And it wasn't just a question of the rules. We also had different outlooks on life. For this reason, I stopped expressing my opinion. It was anyway the complete opposite of that held by the team and, as far as I was concerned, nobody was interested in it.

I tried in vain to go to work in a good mood. At home, in the evenings, I was very tired and sad. I didn't have any idea what else I could do. I thought that I had done everything to improve the situation. Nevertheless, I only felt more ill at ease.

Since I had a fixed-term contract, I wanted to successfully complete my assignment at all costs. I therefore decided to "grin and bear it". It was only once the ordeal was over that I felt better as time passed.

My thoughts, comments and conclusions

In my life, it is not only at work that such situations arise. For some reason, it was embarrassing for me to behave in a way that I considered to be correct. So as not to hurt anyone, for example. Or simply to be the same as everyone else.

In these situations, I tried to adapt to other people. However, my behaviour didn't correspond with my convictions. That's why resistance built up deep within me and grew larger in the process. And when I didn't do anything about it and carried the situation through to its extreme – can you imagine what the outcome was? Precisely! A severe depression or a major dispute. Not a very pleasant prospect, as I'm sure you'll agree?

However, if I was honest, both with myself and with the others, then everyone simply accepted me as I am. If an inner tension did arise, then it was only short-lived.

It therefore makes sense to give thorough consideration to whether you adhere to beliefs that are foreign to you, or whether you remain true to your own convictions...

Your story

Describe a situation from your life that comes to mind in relation to the story you have just read.

Story 12:
What is good and what is bad?

My husband and I once took the decision to sell our apartment and buy a new one. We ultimately wanted to be extraordinarily happy through the change of apartments. We were brimming with feelings of positivity and everything went brilliantly. A buyer was already in place for our apartment and we had also found a new apartment for ourselves. Everything had been settled concerning the move and the handing over of keys, but then…

On the day of the move, it transpired that we still didn't have a key for the new apartment. We nevertheless had to move out of the old one. And now where should we go…?

I went into a state of panic, 'Oh my god! What will we do now?' In contrast, my husband remained absolutely calm and was convinced that we would certainly find a solution, and that the way out was already there.

We moved to our relatives, who lived practically around the corner from our new apartment. Our furniture was stored by a kind-hearted neighbour.

Upon receiving the key to the apartment, we began with the renovation work. I don't want to go into the technical details, but it was very dusty. Ultimately, we were very lucky that our things weren't in the apartment during the renovation.

My thoughts, comments and conclusion

What did we want? We wanted to be both extraordinarily happy with the sale of the old apartment, as well as with the move as a whole. And what did we get in the end? Precisely what we wanted. And the path to the goal? Could I have imagined that, in the end, I would be pleased by what had shocked me at the outset?

How am I to make sense of all of this? Does the path also bring with it surprises that I am only able to understand once I have reached the goal? And, at the same time, that they may not only be pleasant ones – or at least, that's how they seem?

What does this mean? Perhaps it's a good idea to start out by wishing for something that can ultimately bring joy, and then stay as calm as possible on the path to the goal. Especially since not everything that looks bad today will also appear in exactly the same light tomorrow. Incidentally, the same goes for good things too...

Your story

Describe a situation from your life that comes to mind in relation to the story you have just read.

Story 13:
Take advantage of opportunities!

During my hepatitis C therapy my hair began to fall out. So that I could still look good, despite everything, I decided to buy a wig. At the same time, I also wanted to be very satisfied with the purchase.

In a salon, I tried on approximately 20 wigs and selected one of them. However, I couldn't say that I was overjoyed with it. Just as I was about to buy it, I found out from the saleswoman that I could get a prescription for a wig from my doctor. The health insurance could then cover part of the costs. I reserved the wig and discussed it with my doctor. I still had three days before the scheduled doctor's appointment, which is why I asked myself: 'If I still have time, why don't I pay a visit to other salons?'

During these days, my husband and I visited a further three salons where I tried on wigs and selected three more. In the process, I liked each new wig more than the previous one.

In order to make it easier to reach a decision, we took some photos. Looking at them, I came to the conclusion as to which of the hairstyles would work with my hair type and which of the hair colours is the easiest to maintain.

In the end, not only did I have a wig that was in keeping with my wish but I also knew which hairstyles and colours best suit me.

My thoughts, comments and conclusions

What would I have had if I didn't pay a visit to any more salons? A wig, with which I wasn't entirely satisfied. And that would have been all! I can well imagine that such situations had already occurred several times in my life.

Consequently, if something doesn't work, it makes sense to ask oneself, 'What opportunities does this situation present me with?' However, if I had a good opportunity and didn't use it, then it is as though it never existed…

Your story

Describe a situation from your life that comes to mind in relation to the story you have just read.

Story 14:
Listen to your intuition!

My husband and I once went to the library to return some books. It was the last day of the return-by date and we wanted to take them back in time.

Normally, the librarian would scan the books and give us a receipt showing that they had been returned. On this particular day, she merely placed the books to one side.

My husband went through the shelves in order to find something interesting and I waited for him at the counter. I found it odd that the books remained lying on the table without being scanned. My husband then came back, we said goodbye to the librarian and went home.

One week later we received a reminder from the library, stating that a book hadn't been returned and that we must pay a fine. I immediately remembered what had happened at the time and said so to my husband. He said that he also found it odd that we didn't receive a confirmation of the return. Nevertheless, neither of us had said anything about it whilst we were in the library. And now we didn't have any proof that we had returned the book.

My thoughts, comments and conclusions

In this particular case, there was a happy ending – the "missing" book was found. However, time and again I notice that it is better to immediately listen to your intuition. If you leave things to chance, it is questionable as to whether you will be satisfied with the result...

Your story

Describe a situation from your life that comes to mind in relation to the story you have just read.

Story 15:
It's better to die and to be left in peace...

Many years ago I sat in an empty compartment of a suburban train in the evening. A group of drunken youths got in at one of the stops. They wanted me to get out with them at the next stop. Since I had other plans, they had to use force to get me off the train.

I was then on the platform and the train continued on its way. I looked around and realised that I was surrounded by nothing but fields, and that there was nowhere for me to escape. I no longer had any strength after having put up a fight...

My attempt to convince the youths to desist with their plans had ended in a complete failure. They were callous and didn't listen to me at all. In this instant it became clear to me that I was totally on my own and without help of any kind.

'Oh well, so it looks as though today will be my last. Okay, if that's the case, then so be it,' I thought to myself. At this moment I was no longer afraid and agitated. All I felt was a detached calmness within me.

I was supposed to jump from the platform. Since I refused, they pushed me over the edge. At this point, I saw my whole life rush before my eyes, and it was as though everything was over.

I then became aware that I had been dragged somewhere by somebody, and I understood that the end had not yet arrived. One of the youths ordered me to stand up and said that I was to go with him, otherwise he would kill me. In my present situation, this possibility seemed to me to be a much simpler and easier way out. I challenged him to do precisely that. He told me that I wasn't right in the head. The other youth left me lying there and then they all ran away. As I stood up, I saw people in the far distance running towards me to help me.

My thoughts, comments and conclusions

To this day, I have the feeling that it was only my inner calm, cool rationality, indifference, and the fact that I refused to give in to the perpetrators, that helped me. And what could have happened if I had simply been too afraid? I don't even want to think about it.

I also noticed that the inner calm only then came as the last hope of finding external help died away. Can it be that we perhaps have everything that we need within us...?

Speaking of which, I forgot to tell you what I thought about during this period, and in what state I was in. At the time, I didn't know what I was doing on this planet and I had no interest in continuing to live.

Your story

Describe a situation from your life that comes to mind in relation to the story you have just read.

Story 16:
Fortune smiles on the brave!

For a while, during the course of my studies at the technical university, I led a group that was concerned with the design of posters. Our dean had verbally promised me that all of the students from my group would receive a place in the halls of residence.

Following the committee meeting about student accommodation, in which the dean participated, it became clear that several students from my group had not received a place. As the dean was leaving the room, I blocked his path and, in the presence of those gathered, asked, 'How could that happen? You promised me!' He told me that he hadn't given me his word.

Can you imagine how I reacted? I said that I couldn't understand how somebody, who held such a position, could break their word. I assured him that I would only believe written promises in future. At the same time, I suggested that I give up my place in the hall of residence and offer it to a fellow student from my group.

One week later, all of the students from my group – myself included – had a place in the hall of residence.

My thoughts, comments and conclusions

At the time I was very surprised by my reaction. I was afraid of doing something for myself, but my courage knew no bounds for others. I thought, 'If I were to look after myself as much as I look after others, then it would be really beneficial!'

Your story

Describe a situation from your life that comes to mind in relation to the story you have just read.

Story 17:
And just where is the happy medium...?

Whilst studying psychology, I made a really valuable discovery for myself. I saw both my mistakes in my son's upbringing, as well as the possibilities of improving the situation. Inspired by this idea, I decided to immediately put it into practice. Especially because I had always wanted us to understand each other, and to have a close and friendly relationship, but I didn't previously know how to achieve this.

How was it before? If my son had behaved in a way that I had expected, then I saw it as something to be taken for granted. Praise was only something to be given for a special reason. This meant that it happened very rarely. However, if I was dissatisfied with my son's behaviour, and specifically when it concerned anything trivial, then I very frequently had words with him. This led to an argument, sometimes to the use of force and, subsequently, to the worsening of our relationship as well. Ultimately, we both suffered as a result.

After deciding to change the situation, I apologised to my son for my earlier behaviour. He was amazed and shocked. I began to not only see the things that I didn't like, but also those that I had previously taken for granted, namely the pleasant things. The first time, when I praised my son for some small progress at school, he got tears in his eyes. He said that he had never imagined it would ever happen.

My thoughts, comments and conclusions

It transpired that nothing is to be taken for granted! Everything is worthy of my attention: both homework that hasn't been done, as well as homework that has.

It seems that feedback is truly necessary for all of us. In the process, praise is good when it is justified and is given wholeheartedly. Otherwise, who is convinced by it...? Even tiny improvements, if attention is paid to them and they are remarked upon, can provide the motivation to do something greater.

Criticism only makes sense if it is constructive and well-founded. And, indeed, when you concern yourself more with the possibilities for improvement, than with the problem itself.

At the same time, if I feel that something is going wrong, then it is better to react immediately before emotions get out of hand. Otherwise, I don't control them… they control me. And then it's too late for constructive criticism. And nothing good will result from it. Is that what we really need?

Your story

Describe a situation from your life that comes to mind in relation to the story you have just read.

Story 18:
Endlessly positive!

As I began to learn German more intensively, I was very afraid of speaking on the telephone – both of personally making calls and also of accepting a call. Each time I would say to myself, 'I am not afraid, I am not afraid, I am not afraid...' However, for some reason, I became even more afraid. I therefore ran to the library in order to find books on the subject.

In one book I read about the use of positive words. It concerned the fact that certain words generate concrete feelings, which may either help or be detrimental in each situation. At the same time, the unconscious mind ignored the negation such as "not", "un-", "no". It therefore perceived "no fear" as "fear".

'Wow, that can help me!' I thought and decided to replace "no fear" with something positive. I first wanted to find an appropriate synonym, and the right counterpart. I can tell you this was not a particularly easy task. In general, I had the impression that there are more negative words than positive ones. 'That's probably why we live like we do...' I thought.

Whatever the truth is, I found the suitable words. However, it wasn't just one word, but rather a concretely worded goal, which even put me in a good mood. And I began to say to myself, 'I am calm. I understand what is being said to me, and I am able to express and explain my thoughts in German.'

My thoughts, comments and conclusions

If the unconscious mind works in such a way, is it perhaps possible to make use of it? You can then still go from a negative word to a well-worded goal. And why do we so rarely use positive words with negation…? Instead of "sick" we can say "not healthy", instead of "sad" we can say "not happy" etc. And then there is nothing left for the unconscious mind to do than to serve us in our best interests!

Your story

Describe a situation from your life that comes to mind in relation to the story you have just read.

Story 19:
Coincidences are never a coincidence...

Upon receiving the hepatitis C diagnosis, I was convinced that it was a mistake. 'How could I have something like this?' The question left me feeling stunned. Then came the next question, 'Why did I deserve this?' Only later was it clear to me it was no coincidence that I had got this disease. And do you know why?

As soon as I understood that there was no mistake, I decided to cleanse my body in the hope of becoming healthy. Especially because I had previously wanted to undertake a fasting cure. Nevertheless, I had hesitated at the last moment. There was always something that prevented me from doing so: Too much work, holiday and..., and..., and... This time I was immediately prepared and even did the fasting cure! I cleansed my body until there was nothing more to cleanse!

I also gave up smoking back then, which is something I had wanted to do for a long time. Especially since I no longer enjoyed it. However, I was unable to conquer the virus and therefore decided to turn to traditional medicine.

From the very start of the therapy, I had an allergy to the medicine. Among other things, it caused my face to swell up. During this period, our son came to visit us. He said he had recently looked at my old photos and had come to the conclusion that I look the same as I did when I was twenty years old. I immediately wanted to see the photos. He was right! I looked very similar. At this moment, I remembered my wish to look perfect. I wanted a smooth complexion without wrinkles. 'Well, yes, dreams come true!' I thought. 'Am I really bothered by these wrinkles...?'

In the first three months I continued to go to work. However, I had to greatly reduce my hours. Afterwards, my whole skin and also my muscles and lymph nodes were inflamed within a relatively short space of time. It was precisely then, as I was struck down by fever, that I got the idea to write this book. I had spent a whole year thinking about it, but had no idea of what it could be about. And now I didn't just have an idea, but also the time to act upon it...

At some point I gave thought to buying a wig. I wanted to conduct a seminar, but I didn't have much hair on my head. For this reason, I paid a visit to all of the salons in my town. The end result was that I had a wig and knew which hairstyles and hair colours suit me. And then I remembered my old wish to find the right hairstyle and colour.

My thoughts, comments and conclusions

What is it that I want to say? This was not an illness, but rather a goldmine for the fulfilment of my wishes! And what a way for it to happen?! As you can see, these were my own wishes! At the same time, I could have lived very well without a few of them… I would have been able to realise the others myself, also without such a dramatic cause!

I also noticed that there was no mention of my personal wellbeing in any of these wishes. To be honest, it would have been highly appropriate! For it is precisely this that was missing during the treatment – and indeed to a large extent.

I therefore learnt to reflect on whether I precisely need this or something else? And if I want something, then wouldn't it be better to not merely wish for it, but also to act upon it…? Especially if I have the opportunity to do so. Otherwise, it may be that I find myself in a situation in which I am forced to do so. Does it really have to come to this…?

Your story

Describe a situation from your life that comes to mind in relation to the story you have just read.

Story 20:
Love can move mountains!

My husband and my mother once had a very serious quarrel. Neither one even wanted to speak another word with the other. And as for me? What was I supposed to do?

Our friends told us that I must choose between my husband and my mother. And just how could I make this decision when both people were so close to my heart…?

I wanted us all to have a good relationship with each other. Nevertheless, all of my efforts were in vain, since none of us were in a very good humour on this subject.

One evening a Buddhist friend came to pay us a visit. He suggested that I address both with an open heart. He said that love was all that could help. And, do you know what, I believed him.

Once I had calmed down, I decided to speak to both of them again. However, to now do so in a loving way. I don't know where the words came from but, to my surprise, both my husband and my mother understood me this time. It was the first success on the path to restoring peace and mutual understanding in our family.

My thoughts, comments and conclusions

Time and again, I convince myself that the best results can be achieved through love!

Your story

Describe a situation from your life that comes to mind in relation to the story you have just read.

Story 21:
And then along came happiness

As I began to teach, I was particularly thorough in my preparation for seminars. With every assignment, I paid attention to every detail and tried to be prepared for all possible questions. I was very afraid to make a mistake and to deviate from my lesson plan. I feared that I would panic if this happened and thereby make an incompetent impression. I wanted to do everything perfectly.

At each training session, I strictly adhered to the planned sequence and simultaneously concentrated primarily on my professional behaviour. As a result, I was constantly tense. This prevented me from reacting informally and quickly to the group's needs. Although the seminar participants were satisfied, the work didn't give me very much pleasure.

When I moved my attention away from myself and onto my seminar participants and their needs, and allowed myself to make mistakes and to deviate away from the lesson plan, when necessary, the result was the emergence of indescribable happiness. And I wasn't the only one who felt this.

My thoughts, comments and conclusions

I spent a long time thinking about how I actually achieved this. It suddenly became clear to me. I had begun to do what I had previously been afraid of doing. At the same time, I showed love and compassion towards the others. This helped me to relax. And then along came happiness.

Your story

Describe a situation from your life that comes to mind in relation to the story you have just read.

Story 22:
The buck stops here!

I was once a member of a team of trainers who held a two-day seminar in the Crimea. Two of my colleagues and I had return tickets for the same train. I was convinced that the other two knew the departure time of our train. For this reason, I didn't check it myself and instead relied upon the others.

On the day of departure, we were already standing in front of the hotel door when I asked my colleagues what time our train was leaving. And then the inevitable happened – none of us knew the time of departure because we had each relied upon the others. And we then ran to our suitcases to check our tickets.

Do you know how many minutes we had left to get to our train? Approximately five. And we weren't even close to the train station...

My thoughts, comments and conclusions

You probably already know the point that I wish to make...? If you simply rely upon yourself, then everything is certain to work out!

Your story

Describe a situation from your life that comes to mind in relation to the story you have just read.

Story 23:
Over and over again...

My colleague, with whom I very much enjoyed running seminars, once informed me before Christmas that I would work with someone else in the coming year, since she had signed an employment contract for the year ahead.

I went into a panic and asked myself, 'How should I manage it without her? And what if it doesn't work with someone else?' I therefore told her that my wish would be to continue to conduct seminars with her in the following year.

I found what she told me to be simply brilliant. She said that nobody knew what is best for each of us and recommended to me, 'We can wish each other that the coming year holds only the best for each of us.'

I clung firmly to this idea. And whenever I felt afraid of the future, I repeated this thought in my head.

In the following year I only conducted one seminar with her. I conducted the rest with two other trainers. And these collaborations were also marvellous. I later had the opportunity to work with her again.

My thoughts, comments and conclusions

Can it be that clinging to someone results in a dead end? Isn't it better to wish myself, as well as those close to me, the best for each of us?

And if we are afraid of the future, doesn't it make more sense to replace the fear with the wish that the future holds the best for us...? And, namely, over and over again... ;-)

Your story

Describe a situation from your life that comes to mind in relation to the story you have just read.

Story 24:
Allow yourself to be inspired!

One spring I visited a botanical garden with my husband and my son. It was there that I saw magnolia trees for the first time in my life. I found them to be so beautiful that I was overcome with joy.

Whenever I recalled these beautiful trees, I had a feeling as wonderful as back then. And do you know what? The trees began to accompany me.

My family and I moved. To my complete amazement, in my town I saw a couple of magnolia trees in the spring. This was simply wonderful!

And where do I live now? In a town in which I am entirely surrounded by this unbelievable beauty and by which I continue to be fascinated!

My thoughts, comments and conclusions

Allow yourself to be inspired! We attract everything that brings us joy.

Your story

Describe a situation from your life that comes to mind in relation to the story you have just read.

Story 25:
The finger points at the moon

My family loves activity holidays and loves travelling. For this reason, my husband, my son and I have a very clear idea of how preparations for such a holiday can be undertaken more easily and comfortably. Since there are two programmers in our family, we decided to develop a web application that is intended to ease such holiday preparations.

The first step towards the goal was clear, and we set off towards it with a great deal of commitment. We initially made impressive progress. And then came new ideas, and indeed one after the other, which blew our project out of proportion. We went into such great detail that we lost sight of our goal in the process.

Since we didn't see any light at the end of the tunnel, our enthusiasm faded greatly. It is not unlimited, whether we believe it or not... As a result, there was always something that kept us from working, until the project eventually came to a standstill. It was during this period that I was diagnosed with hepatitis C and my family began to take care of me. It was no longer about the project, but rather about me...

My thoughts, comments and conclusions

A couple of moments particularly stand out for me.

I don't know how it is for you, but I normally see just one step to my goal. As long as I don't take it, then I don't know how things are going to progress. Therefore, when a step is clear, doesn't it make sense to first undertake it without wracking our brains about what is going to come next...?

On the path to the goal, I find it helpful to always keep my eyes on the goal itself. Otherwise, I can lose my way and completely forget where I actually want to get to. This is similar to the Zen saying about the finger that is pointing to the moon. The path is only a means to achieving a goal; it is only a finger. If I focus my eyes on the finger, how can I see the moon...?

Your story

Describe a situation from your life that comes to mind in relation to the story you have just read.

Story 26:
Boomerang

During one holiday, my husband and I jogged along the ocean almost every morning. One morning, whilst jogging, I saw a bunker dating back to World War Two.

I said to my husband that we didn't have any photos of this kind. My husband replied that he didn't have any intention of photographing it. He even added that there were sufficient beautiful and peaceful motives. 'Oh well, then it's not to be,' I thought.

The next morning, we saw a man meditating on the bunker. 'Wow! Such a building and it looks absolutely peaceful,' my husband said. In the embrasure of another bunker, we then saw a cat that was casually taking a walk. 'That would have been a beautiful photo,' he commented.

The odd thing was that, right up to the day of our departure, there were no further motives of this kind.

My thoughts, comments and conclusions

Has something of the kind ever happened to you? I mean, where you have so vehemently rejected something, and then the situation has changed to such a degree that you have done it anyway?

I have experienced this on many occasions in my life. I have therefore come to the conclusion that everything, to which I react emotionally, comes back to me like a boomerang. And the more emotion I put into it, irrespective of whether it is positive or negative, the more likely it is that it will happen.

Therefore, if I wholeheartedly negate something, the negation falls away and only the act remains. I think you can well imagine what happened to me when I wholeheartedly said something along the lines of 'I'm not going to do it', 'I don't want it' etc.

Your story

Describe a situation from your life that comes to mind in relation to the story you have just read.

Story 27:
My decision – my responsibility!

When our son had almost finished his final secondary school examinations, he informed us of his wish to be an actor. My husband and I said, 'If you want to, then give it a try.' My mother was against it, saying, 'You and your husband are crazy to support such an idea! Do you want to say that it's a good career? Can you have family and money in the process? There are only theatre tours. And not everyone becomes a star!' Everything that she said made sense, but...

I remembered my childhood, when two school classmates and I wanted to train in legal studies. Our parents were initially in favour of it. A survey was then carried out by our form teacher. It concerned whether each of us wanted to participate in a training course or to stay in the school. And we expressed our plans honestly.

Our form teacher nevertheless had misgivings about our plans, which is why my friend's mother and my mother changed their opinion after the parent's evening. They were completely opposed to the idea. We were two young girls, and a specialist college of this kind only existed in another town. Since our parents wanted to protect us, they wouldn't allow us to undergo a training course elsewhere. As a result, neither of us pursued this career. Although I later got degrees in other academic areas, I also studied a statutory and legal foundation course in the process.

My friend is total satisfied with her life today. Nevertheless, many years later, she told me that we would have made very good lawyers, if we had chosen this career back then...

My thoughts, comments and conclusions

Who knows what talent is hidden within each of us...? If you don't try it, then you'll never find out. And what is the purpose of a family? I believe it is to provide one another with support. It is one thing to express and substantiate a personal opinion. However, wouldn't it be better if each individual were to make their own decisions...?

Your story

Describe a situation from your life that comes to mind in relation to the story you have just read.

Story 28: Majority

In my family, it used to be the case that the majority opinion was taken into account in the planning of holidays. Therefore, if two had agreed in favour of something, the third had no choice but to fall into line with the majority vote. In this way, each of us has been in the minority role. Has something like this also happened to you at one time?

During one holiday, my husband said, 'It's been quite a while since I enjoyed a holiday as much as I did when I was a child. I am now on holiday, and I would like to do what I enjoy. But I don't have the enthusiasm or, rather, the enthusiasm that I used to have.'

I then asked him precisely what had given him this idea. And he answered, 'I felt sad as I was watching windsurfers on the waves today. I have been practising this sport for years now, but I still can't windsurf like them. I often wanted to pursue this sport, but instead we went hiking because that's what the majority wanted.'

My thoughts, comments and conclusions

So, I then gave this some thought. What is the point of a holiday if one person is dissatisfied with it...? Wouldn't it make more sense if we went on holiday to a place where there is something to suit everyone? I believe it is possible to find such a place, if the wish is there. What do you think?

And perhaps this doesn't just apply to a holiday, but also for other joint plans...? Is it not better if all those involved are completely satisfied with a common purchase, for example?

Your story

Describe a situation from your life that comes to mind in relation to the story you have just read.

Story 29:
'Why?' Is that a question or a wish?

There were sometimes participants in my group, who looked 15-20 years younger than they were. At the same time, they continually complained that they were in a bad shape and were frequently being put on sick leave.

I simply couldn't understand it and continually asked myself, 'Why?' After all, they looked absolutely healthy and young. I would have like to look so good when I was their age.

During my hepatitis C therapy, I had an allergic reaction to medication and my face became swollen. My colleagues noticed that I looked much younger. At this very moment, the reason became clear to me.

And I then questioned whether I had asked myself 'Why?' questions at any other time in my life, and namely with so much emotion...

My thoughts, comments and conclusions

I came to the conclusion that, by asking such a question, you can find yourself in a similar situation. It is then that you can best understand 'Why...?' I now give some thought as to whether I really need an answer to every 'Why?' question...

Your story

Describe a situation from your life that comes to mind in relation to the story you have just read.

Story 30:
Bless you!

When my father-in-law got annoyed with someone, he said, 'Bless you!' instead of cursing. Even back then, I liked this approach very much. Nevertheless, it is only now, many years later, that it has become clear to me what it embodies.

If I am in a bad mood or unhappy with someone, for example, I can let a curse slip out. However, assuming that everything I say emotionally comes back to me, then things don't look quite so rosy. Don't you agree? And, namely, not only vis-à-vis the others but also to myself.

As I remembered my father-in-law's response, a thought came to my head, 'Can it perhaps become a habit to say something good, when I am filled with negative emotions? If there is already so much energy within me, doesn't it then make sense to steer it in an advantageous direction?' I began to act accordingly from this point onwards. It would be simply great if it were always to work.

Once, whilst out jogging, I began to preach to my son about how he should organise his life. And he told me with a smile, 'Mum, you can begin by focusing on everything that you wish for yourself. You have ample energy for all that you need!'

My thoughts, comments and conclusions

If something annoys me and emotions rise to the surface, isn't it then better to concentrate my thoughts upon things that please me...? And if that all comes back to me, then I will be happy about it!

Your story

Describe a situation from your life that comes to mind in relation to the story you have just read.

Story 31:
A conversation with the shadows

Previously, when preparing for a discussion, I conducted a dialogue beforehand in my head. It didn't matter what the subject was... whether it was an interview or another meeting that was important for me. And I began to talk to myself, 'If they ask me that, then I will answer like this. And then they will say that... And I will reply with the following...'

This really helped me when I was preparing for an interview. However, it didn't really support me for other kinds of discussions. And do you know why? I prepared for a specific sequence, which only hindered me instead of helping me, since the discussion went very differently in reality.

For this reason, I decided to change my approach. I began to not concentrate on my discussion, but rather on the result that I wanted. I therefore focused my attention on the goal and on my inner state. It was about having a friendly approach to the dialogue partner and the inner attitude that, irrespective of the result of the discussion, everything would work out to my advantage. This helped me to relax and to find my inner calm.

From this moment onwards I have been able to behave very naturally at each meeting, which is something that has greatly helped me in every kind of situation.

My thoughts, comments and conclusions

I can't tell you whether a conversation with the shadows is really necessary, but attention should always be paid to personal goals and inner attitude. At the same time, this doesn't only concern a planned meeting, but also the day ahead, the holiday and so on.

Your story

Describe a situation from your life that comes to mind in relation to the story you have just read.

Story 32:
Are you in harmony with yourself...?

I once had a nightmare: There was something wrong with our car, and yet my husband continued to drive it for his work. In the evening, two of his friends came to me and told me that he would never return home. I was so afraid that I immediately woke up.

In the morning, my husband actually did want to drive with the car, despite frequent problems with the engine. I was seized by panic and tried to dissuade him from driving. But I was unsuccessful. For this reason, I drove with him in order to change the situation that had appeared in my dream.

The car came to a standstill on a sharp uphill bend and the engine failed to start up. As we were considering what we could do, I saw my husband's friends nearby... the ones who had also appeared in my dream. With their help we managed to start the car. And everything worked out well.

My thoughts, comments and conclusions

I have often applied this strategy in order to change situations that I have seen in my dream. This got me thinking that it only concerns a possible future, and nothing else. I can decide whether it suits me or not. Therefore, let's assume that something in my dream makes me afraid. However, in reality, if I change the situation or my behaviour, then the result changes as well.

There are also dreams that are repeated from time to time over the years, and which bring with them the same sense of pain. These dreams may appear different, but they have the same meaning and the same protagonists. I used to firmly believe that I couldn't change anything in dreams such as these. However, I now think differently about them. Have you ever given it some thought...?

Your story

Describe a situation from your life that comes to mind in relation to the story you have just read.

Story 33:
Peace and comfort!

When something unsettles me, I ask myself, 'What would make you happy in this situation?'

Sometimes it was the case that, irrespective of what I thought about, all of my ideas were connected with unpleasant emotions. For this reason, I continued to look for other possibilities in order to find a goal. At the same time, I was constantly in an unpleasant state of mind in which I had negative emotions. Does this sound familiar?

I was in this state. Therefore, in order to distract myself from my thoughts about a specific question, for which I was unable to find an answer, I began to listen to beautiful music, to meditate and to practise different, pleasant activities. However, none of this helped me and I became ill.

I have now changed my approach in the formulation of my goals. I only wish myself something that is of benefit to all concerned. For, based upon my experience, the core of the failure lies in self-centred thought.

If I am unable to imagine a concrete goal, then I begin with the following sentence, 'I am thrilled by how I live'. This thought brings me joy. I go into detail until I sense positive feelings and my goal corresponds to my conviction that all those concerned will benefit in the process.

And how do you formulate your goals?

My thoughts, comments and conclusions

What do I wish to add to this? When I am relaxed and filled with positive emotions, it is then a good time to ask myself questions such as, 'What do I need in order to be happy? What pleased me today? What would I like to experience tomorrow?' and so on.

I have such thoughts before going to bed and directly afterwards, when I'm listening to music whilst jogging, sunbathing or tidying up etc. You undoubtedly also have such moments during the day, in which you are relaxed and feel good ;-)

Your story

Describe a situation from your life that comes to mind in relation to the story you have just read.

CHAPTER 2:

FROM GRATITUDE TO MANIFESTATION

Light at the end of the tunnel

After writing the final story, I compiled a list with goals that inspired me. Thanks to all that I learnt from the stories, I became convinced that I can achieve these goals, even if they aren't formulated in concrete terms.

At the time, I summarised my goals in the following single sentence:

I am thrilled by how I live!

In detail, my sub-goals were as follows:

I am grateful that:

- *I maintain inner calm and that I live in harmony with myself*
- *I am filled with love and that I radiate love vis-à-vis others*
- *I feel good, absolutely healthy and physically fit*
- *I love myself as I am, and others as they are*
- *I am happy to allow personal freedom, both for myself and also for others*
- *my relationship with other people is a true pleasure and enrichment for all concerned*
- *my behaviour and my thoughts make me happy*
- *I enjoy where, how and with whom I live*
- *I love developing my talent and benefitting from my professional life*
- *my goals inspire me*
- *I am thrilled by what I do, and by where, how and with whom I do it*
- *the results of my activity make me happy and enrich me, as well as my clients and my partner*
- *I very much enjoy realising my projects and supporting others that I like*

- *the paths to my goals are very easy, pleasant and harmonious*
- *I believe in success and react very calmly to all that takes place!*

In addition, I wish the absolute best for myself, for those who are close to me, for my colleagues, my acquaintances and everyone living on this planet!

A brief report 10 years later

Ten years later, I would like to summarise what I have achieved of the aforementioned goals.

I'll start with the main goal: *I am thrilled by how I live!*

Today I can say that I am a happy person because I love everything in my life and my life brings me a lot of joy.

Now I'm moving on to the individual parts of my main goal.

I am grateful that:

I maintain inner calm and that I live in harmony with myself.

I can say that I have achieved this goal. Sometimes I feel uncomfortable, but I see negative feelings as indicators that something is going wrong. As soon as I understand the cause of the problem and know how to solve it, peace of mind returns.

To achieve this goal, I had to learn a lot. This included, among other things, to:

- rely on myself
- solve problems as they arise
- overcome fears
- repair relationships
- allow myself and others to make mistakes
- work with negative thoughts and emotions
- use dreams to correct my intentions

Avoiding news reports on TV and the internet also plays a big role, since it contains a lot of negative information that is amplified by sound and vision. For this reason, I prefer to read the news.

I am filled with love and that I radiate love vis-à-vis others.

When I formulated this goal, I wanted to replace the negative feelings, caused by various fears, with something positive. I couldn't imagine anything more pleasant than love.

Thanks to this goal, I also started to separate people from their behaviour. In most cases, I am able to treat people with love. If I criticise someone it's not about the person, but about their specific actions.

I feel good, absolutely healthy and physically fit.

During this time, I achieved a lot in this area. In addition to the strength training that I had already been doing, I added stretching, which significantly improved my posture and flexibility.

I switched to veganism for ethical reasons. The plant-based diet was not only healthy, as the results of the check-ups at my GP proved, but to my surprise it was also very tasty.

To give my body more time to regenerate, I switched to decaffeinated coffee and replaced teas that have a stimulating effect, such as black and green tea, with herbal and fruit teas.

I also switched to non-alcoholic drinks and was really surprised to find there is not only non-alcoholic beer, but also wine, my favourite martini and even gin.

The inner peace that dominated me also had a positive effect on my health. For example, I managed to normalise my thyroid gland without medication after being diagnosed with thyroiditis.

I love myself as I am, and others as they are.

I used to compare myself to others all the time. This had not only applied to my appearance and abilities, but also to every activity I had undertaken. It was only when I realised that everyone is unique that I stopped striving to be like or even better than others. Now I like to be myself, and enjoy what I do, because I'm paying attention to my innate abilities.

I had also been critical of my own mistakes and those of others. Once I had allowed myself to make mistakes, I began to treat other people's mistakes with empathy.

I am happy to allow personal freedom, both for myself and also for others.

In a discussion with an acquaintance of mine, whose opinions differed from my own, we once touched on the subject of war and peace. We agreed, at least in theory, on the principle of peaceful co-existence, according to which everyone is free to live as they wish, as long as this does not infringe on the freedoms of others to live as they wish. In other words, I live within my view of the world and allow others to live within theirs, which differs from mine, and react calmly to this.

The more I thought about this principle, the more calmly I reacted to other people's opinions and actions, even if I felt they were wrong. Sometimes the old thought pattern came to the fore, but less often and not as intensely as in the past. I realised I am only responsible for my own beliefs and actions, and that other people are responsible for both their view of the world and their own behaviour.

I used to try to convince others that I was right. Today, I limit myself to expressing my opinion. Whether the other person finds something useful in it or not is up to them. Incidentally, I do this for my own peace of mind so that I don't later blame myself for having been able to do something for a person but not doing it.

My relationship with other people is a true pleasure and enrichment for all concerned.

Thanks to this goal, I reflected on my relationships with other people. I stopped maintaining the relationships that were only sustained by my initiative, and many of them dissolved on their own. I managed to normalise some of the relationships in which either I or the other person felt uncomfortable, and I had to end some of the relationships.

To maintain balance in relationships, I have to be constantly vigilant.

My behaviour and my thoughts make me happy.

When I formulated this wish, I wasn't always sure how to behave in difficult situations with my loved ones. I was afraid of the consequences of my actions because I didn't know where they might lead. My dreams and my desire for equality in relationships helped me to solve this problem.

When it comes to dreams, I went to bed at night with the intention of doing something specific the next day. In the morning I made a decision whether to do it or not, based on my dreams. The desire for equality helped me to recognise and eliminate any imbalances in my relationships.

As for my thoughts, I immediately replaced the negative thoughts that came to my mind – for example, fears about the future – with the opposite i.e. positive thoughts. Thanks to this technique, my mind is dominated by positive thoughts.

I enjoy where, how and with whom I live.

I fell in love at first sight with the city where I now live. I feel like I was born and raised here, which indicates how comfortable I feel in this city. In the meantime, we bought a property and moved to another neighbourhood, which I like even better than the previous one.

In the beginning, my husband and I had a pretty clear idea of the property we wanted to buy. Then we asked ourselves whether that wasn't a limitation. So, we formulated our goal in such a way that we focussed on the feeling we wanted to have, rather than the details. In the end, we bought a property that exceeded our expectations in every respect. I'm doing what I enjoy and living with the man I love.

I love developing my talent and benefitting from my professional life.

I consciously combined my talents and my wealth into one goal so that I could not only do what I enjoy, but also earn a good living doing it. During this time, I became involved in three business projects initiated by our family. Two of them turned out to be unprofitable, so we ended them after a while to focus our attention on a promising project. This enabled my husband and I to organise a passive income for ourselves.

My goals inspire me.

It's true. I only choose goals that inspire me.

I am thrilled by what I do, and by where, how and with whom I do it.

Here, too, everything corresponds to reality. This applies to both work and leisure.

The results of my activity make me happy and enrich me, as well as my clients and my partner.

I can definitely say this is the case for me. As far as customers and partners are concerned, I have the impression that we have a mutually beneficial working relationship.

I very much enjoy realising my projects and supporting others that I like.

During these years, I only worked on projects that I felt good about.

The paths to my goals are very easy, pleasant and harmonious.

Most of them were just like that. But there were also some that were not so easy and sometimes unpleasant.

I believe in success and react very calmly to all that takes place!

I achieved the main goal I set myself when writing the book. Now I am enthusiastic about the way in which I live. Furthermore, in most cases, I am able to react calmly to what is happening and to calm down quickly when I get upset. Understanding that it harms my health and helps no one when I worry helps me to do this.

PART II:
Roadmap to Happiness

Co-author
Stanislav Turchyn

CHAPTER 3:

INTRODUCTION TO THE ROADMAP

I used to think that being happy meant having everything I love. I then realised that this idea of happiness made it an unattainable goal, since there was always more of what I loved than what I had. Yet I wanted to be happy right now.

I later realised that, in order to be happy, it is not necessary to own everything that fascinates me. It is enough to love everything that exists in my life. This thought made me realise that happiness doesn't lie somewhere over the horizon, but rather right next to me. Therefore, in order to be happy, I only have to change what I don't like about my life and keep the things that bring me joy.

My approach is the result of analysing my practical experience. It comprises a step-by-step guide with three steps and four basic practices for working with problems, wishes and goals, feelings and emotions, as well as dreams.

By "wishes" I mean everything that I want but am currently, for whatever reason, unwilling or unable to take steps to achieve. As soon as I understand at least one step and am ready to act, the wish becomes my goal.

The current situation is analysed in the first step, the affirmations for a happy life are formulated in the second step and, in the third step, the steps to the goal are planned and implemented (Figure 1 "Overview of the roadmap"). All the techniques used are explained with examples from my life, which are described in the first part of this book.

The approach is helpful in:

- appreciating everything that brings joy in life
- recognising the causes of problems and finding possible solutions
- transforming problems into wishes and goals
- finding a way out of seemingly hopeless situations
- formulating your wishes and goals, even if you don't know exactly what you want
- taking steps towards the goal and correcting them if necessary

- achieving goals, even in uncertain circumstances
- focusing on the good things in the here and now, as well as on the goals you are striving for
- reducing the number of negative feelings and thoughts, and making negative emotions work for you
- using your dreams to correct your intentions

Step-by-Step Guide

Step 1: Analysis of the current situation

Step 2: Creation of a vision for a happy life

Step 3: Taking action

Basic Practices

Working with problems

Working with affirmations

Working with feelings and emotions

Working with dreams

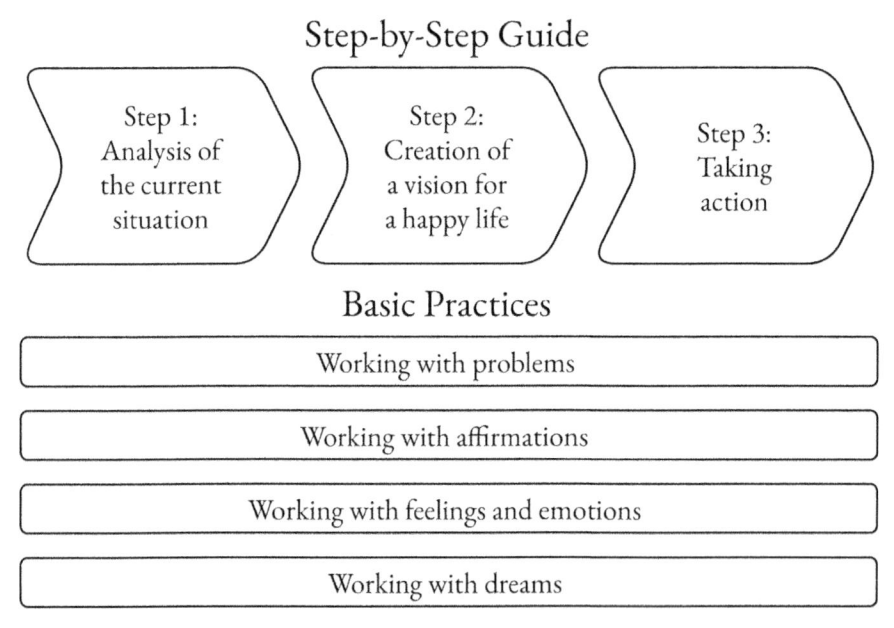

Figure 1 Overview of the roadmap

I use this approach constantly because there is always something in my life that I want to keep. There are always new wishes and goals, but also discomfort, which helps me to recognise exactly what I need to change in order to feel at ease.

Before going into the following chapters in detail, I would like to highlight the most important points of my approach (Figure 2 "Overview of the step-by-step guide in detail").

Step 1: Analysis of your current situation

The first step not only offers you the opportunity to think about what you are grateful for in life, what you wish for and what makes you uncomfortable, but also to transform problems into wishes and goals.

The basic practice "Working with problems" is used to analyse discomfort and helps you to understand the causes of problems and discover possible solutions.

The basic practice "Working with dreams" enables you to recognise unresolved problems.

The basic practice "Working with feelings and emotions" helps you to use negative emotions to your advantage and to deal with fears.

Step 2: Creation of a vision for a happy life

The second step gives you the opportunity to formulate affirmations that describe all aspects of your happy life.

The basic practice "Working with affirmations" is added in the second step, when a "My happy life" list has already been created, and helps you to keep your attention focussed on your wishes and goals.

Step 3: Taking action

The third step allows you to plan and execute the steps to achieve the desired goals, make changes if necessary and, if possible, set deadlines for achieving the goals and steps.

The basic practice "Working with dreams" enables you to use dreams to correct your intentions.

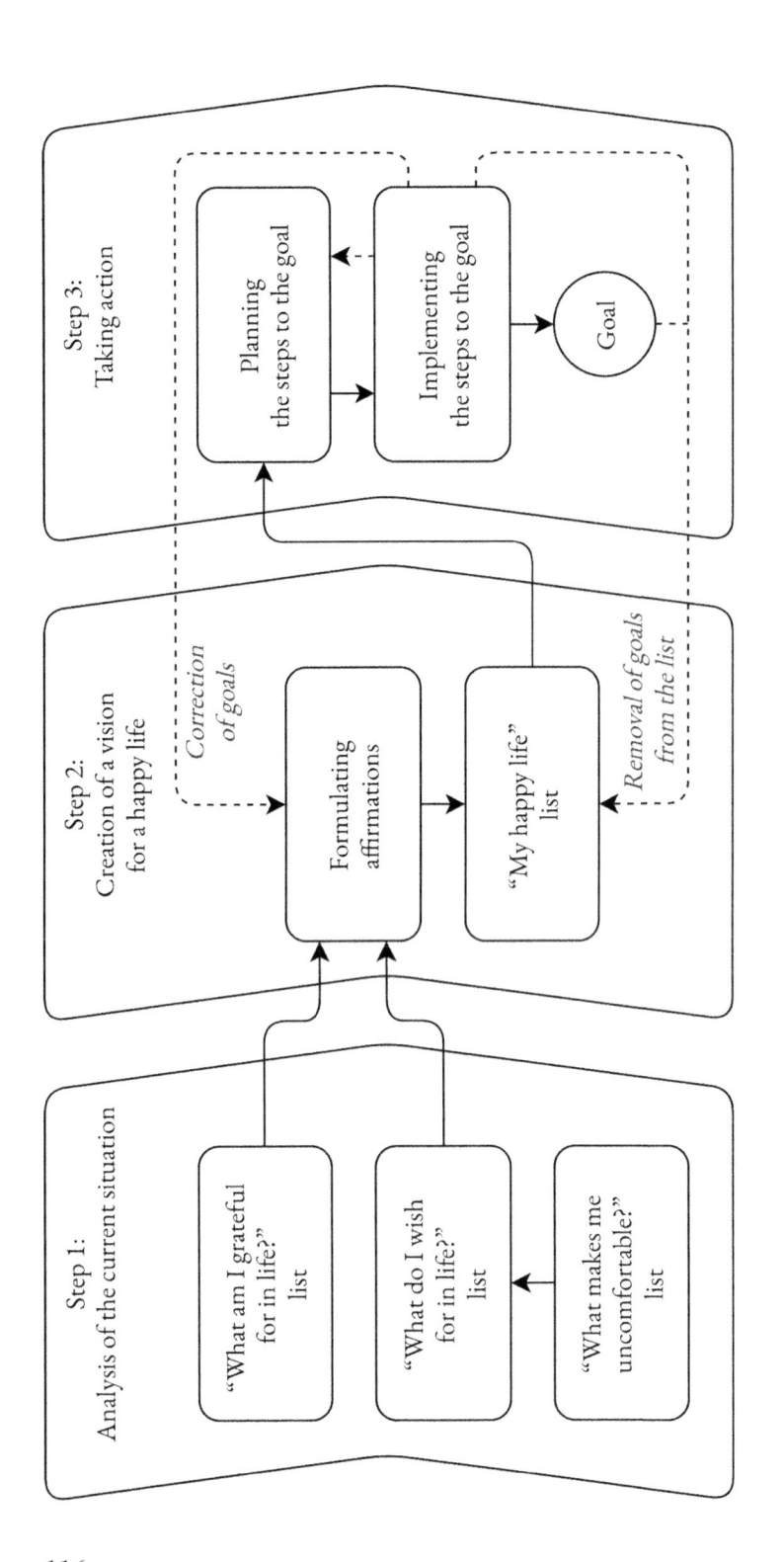

Figure 2 Overview of the step-by-step guide in detail

CHAPTER 4:
A STEP-BY-STEP GUIDE

Step 1:
Analysis of the current situation

The roadmap begins with an analysis of the current situation (Figure 1 "Overview of the roadmap"). In this step I create three lists (Figure 3 "Step 1: Analysis of the current situation"):

- what am I grateful for in life?
- what do I wish for in life?
- what makes me uncomfortable?

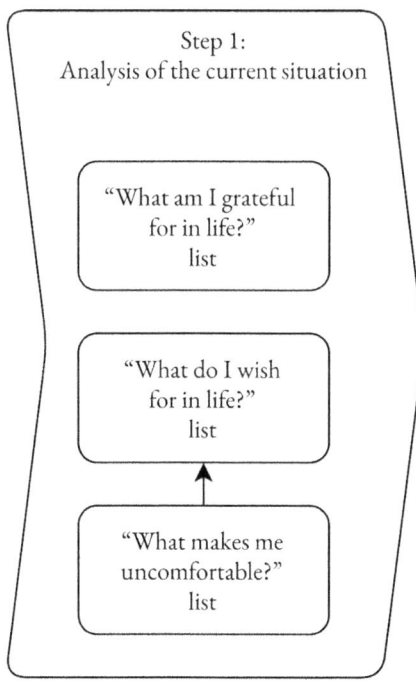

Figure 3 Step 1: Analysis of the current situation

What am I grateful for in life?

Thanks to my observations, I came to the conclusion that as long as I wish for something good, I will get it ("Story 4: Can we all win...? Of course!"). For this reason, I made a list of all the things that bring me joy in all areas of my life (health, family, relationships, finances, professional activities, hobbies, etc.) and what I am grateful for.

Here are some examples from my list, which appear in "Chapter 2: From Gratitude to Manifestation", in the section "Light at the end of the tunnel":

I am grateful that:

- *I enjoy where, how, and with whom I live*
- *I love developing my talents and benefitting from my professional life*

> **Exercise 1:**
>
> Make a list of what you are grateful for ("Chapter 6: Your Gratitude and Manifestation Journal", in the section "What am I grateful for in life?").

What do I wish for in life?

In moments when I am relaxed and full of positive emotions, I ask myself not only what I am grateful for, but also what else I would wish for. The answers to this question are the basis for my list "What do I wish for in life?" Here is an example:

I want to feel good, absolutely healthy and physically fit.

When I analysed various situations in my life, I realised that everything I reacted to emotionally became my goals. This applied both to conscious goals, i.e. all the things I wanted, and to unconscious goals – my emotionally charged statements.

Below are some examples of such statements and subsequent events:

Although, as a child, I categorically claimed that I would never learn German, many years later I was forced by circumstances to learn the language ("Story 6: Never say never!").

One day, my husband flatly refused to take a photo of me on a bunker because he didn't like military objects. The very next day, to our surprise, the bunkers appeared in front of us in such a way that he wanted to photograph them ("Story 26: Boomerang").

The first time I saw magnolias, I was fascinated by their beauty. Now I live in a city where they inspire me at every turn ("Story 24: Allow yourself to be inspired!").

I would never have thought you could get an answer to the question 'Why?' when you find yourself in a similar situation ("Story 29: 'Why?' Is that a question or a wish?").

My absolute fear of speaking in front of an audience ultimately led me to become a teacher ("Story 9: It makes me afraid...? Try it!").

Thanks to these observations, I came to the conclusion that the more emotion I put into something, be it negative or positive, the more likely it is that this very thing will occur. This also applies to my reaction to jokes, stories that happened to other people, etc.

For this reason, I reformulate emotionally charged statements, which I want to avoid being realised, into positively formulated wishes and goals. I use two approaches to work with these wishes and goals.

The first approach is that, immediately after a negative statement, while the emotions are still strong, I reformulate it into the opposite, positively formulated wish and keep saying it until I feel calmer. This approach is used once. It is explained in detail in "Chapter 5: Basic Practices", in the section "Working with feelings and emotions".

In the second approach, I work regularly with a positively formulated wish or goal. To do this, I put it on a list "What do I wish for in life?".

Finally, I would like to make one more point. When I choose wishes and goals, I make sure they don't contradict each other. Here is an example:

On the one hand, I always wanted to be healthy but, on the other, I also wanted to have firm facial skin without wrinkles. I paid much more attention to the desire to look young than the desire to be healthy. In the end, I did look young. However, this happened during my hepatitis C therapy, when my face swelled up due to the medication and I felt really unwell ("Story 19: Coincidences are never a coincidence...").

As a result, I corrected my wish. It now reads as follows: 'I am grateful that I feel good, absolutely healthy and physically fit' ("Chapter 2: From Gratitude to Manifestation", in the section "Light at the end of the tunnel").

> **Exercise 2:**
>
> Make a list of what you want to achieve in life ("Chapter 6: Your Gratitude and Manifestation Journal", in the section "What do I wish for in life?").

What makes me uncomfortable?

If I feel uncomfortable with something, I analyse the problem and turn it into a wish. I start by analysing the problem, which is described in detail in "Chapter 5: Basic Practices", in the section "Working with problems".

How I deal with my fears is explained in "Chapter 5: Basic Practices", in the section "Working with feelings and emotions".

I would also like to point out that dreams help me to become aware of unresolved problems. There is more on this in "Chapter 5: Basic Practices", in the section "Working with dreams".

As soon as I find out what is causing me discomfort, and identify the root cause of the problem, I ask myself the question, 'What would bring me joy?'.

Finally, I get a list of wishes from my problem list, which I also add to my list "What do I wish for in life?".

As an example, I would like to mention a problem and the wishes transformed from it, which is described in detail in "Story 3: When dreams come true..." and "Story 8: I don't know what I want – I don't want what I know...":

I simply didn't feel like doing my job anymore because it was difficult to get along with some colleagues and unmotivated customers.

The wishes transformed from this problem were as follows:

- *I am thrilled by what I do, and by where, how and with whom I do it*
- *my customers, colleagues, employer and I are very satisfied with my performance*

Exercise 3:

Use a notebook for this exercise or create notes in digital format.

Learn to transform problems into wishes and goals.

Make a list of what makes you uncomfortable.

From the list, choose one problem that bothers you the most.

Analyse this problem (Exercise 6 in "Chapter 5: Basic Practices", in the section "Working with problems").

Imagine that the problem has already been resolved. Describe the situation in which you feel comfortable. Formulate one or more wishes and add them to the list "What do I wish for in life?" ("Chapter 6: Your Gratitude and Manifestation Journal", in the section "What do I wish for in life?").

Repeat this for other problems from your list.

Step 2:
Creation of a vision for a happy life

After analysing the current situation and making lists of "What am I grateful for?" and "What do I wish for in life?", I move on to formulating affirmations in detail (Figure 4 "Step 2: Creation of a vision for a happy life").

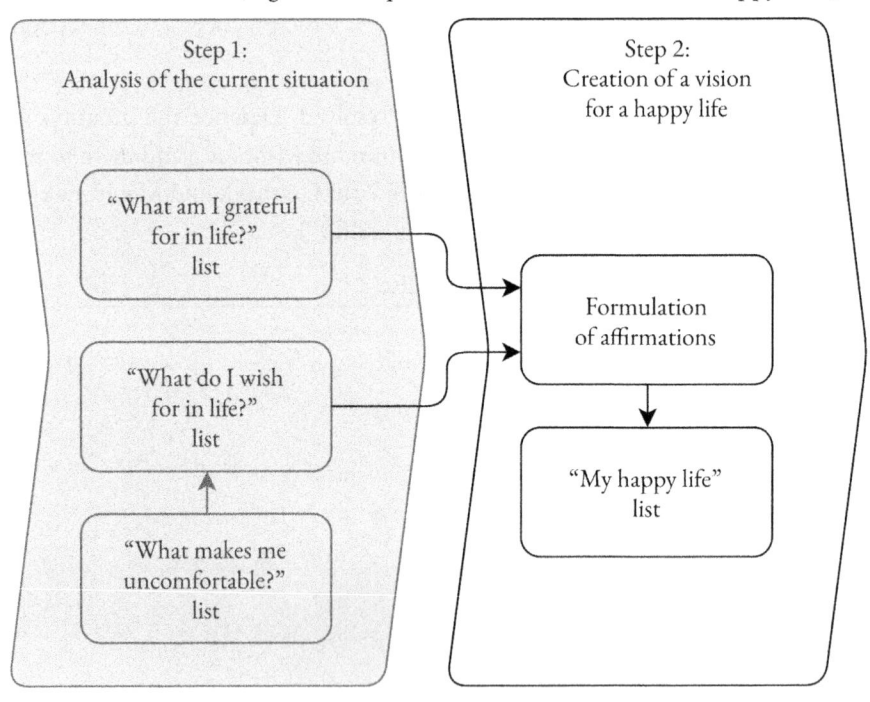

Figure 4 Step 2: Creation of a vision for a happy life

As a result, I create a list "My happy life".

I would like to use the situation with the neighbour from "Story 10: Making things worse for the better" as a key example of how I approach the formulation of my affirmations.

I formulate my affirmations in the present tense, as if they had already been realised. They are listed in "Chapter 2: From Gratitude to Manifestation", in the section "Light at the end of the tunnel".

> *In the example with the neighbour, my goal was defined as follows: 'I am very satisfied with my comfortable flat and the pleasant relationships with my neighbours'.*

When formulating affirmations, I ask myself a number of questions:

Can I visualise a specific goal? If not, I start with a general sentence, for example, 'I am thrilled by how I live'. This thought should make me happy. I only go into detail as long as I feel comfortable with it ("Story 33: Peace and comfort!").

> *The only wording that I had a good feeling about was the following: 'I am very satisfied with my comfortable flat and the pleasant relationships with my neighbours'. That's why I decided in favour of this version.*

Do I succeed in wishing for what is beneficial for all concerned? If not, I concentrate only on myself and my goal, without wishing anything bad for others ("Story 4: Can we all win...? Of course!").

> *In the wording 'I am very satisfied with my comfortable flat and the pleasant relationships with my neighbours', I focused only on myself and my own well-being. I tried to avoid thinking about my neighbour because it triggered extremely unpleasant feelings in me. Although I found it difficult to wish her something nice, I still wanted to do so. I then found a solution by starting to wish that everyone was doing well. This wording also included those people who evoked negative emotions in me, when I thought about them, and yet it made me feel good (last paragraph in the section "Light at the end of the tunnel" in chapter 2 "From Gratitude to Manifestation").*

Is my wish dependent on the actions of another person? Do I want a certain person to do something for me without telling them? Such wishes are the reason for unjustified hopes, and unfulfilled hopes lead to disappointment. That's why I speak openly about my wish with the person I want something ("Story 23: Over and over again..."). In the past, I was often surprised to find that I got what I wanted from someone other than the person from whom I had initially wanted it.

Am I clinging to someone else with my wish? If so, I change the wording and wish for the best for both myself and the person I want to be with. After all, I can't know what's best for each of us.

> *In the case of my colleague from "Story 23: Over and over again...", I wanted to continue working with her the following year, even though she had completely different plans. Thanks to the conversation with her, I formulated my wish differently: 'I'm very happy that everything went so well for both me and my colleague'.*

Can I harm someone with my wish? Do I want to force the other person to give up their wishes ("Story 27: My decision – my responsibility!")?

In this case, I would like to refer back to the examples with my neighbour and my colleague. In the phrases 'I am very satisfied with my comfortable flat and the pleasant relationships with my neighbours' and 'I am very happy that everything has gone well for both me and my colleague', there is no desire to harm them or make them give up their intentions.

If I want to help someone, I ask myself, 'Can it hurt me?'. In this way, I can avoid creating a problem for myself by solving someone else's problem ("Story 10: Making things worse for the better").

In the situation with the neighbour, it all started with my desire to help her. By making concessions to the neighbour, I brought discomfort into my family's life.

Are the wishes of all parties involved taken into account in the common goals, so that everyone is satisfied with the result?

In this case, I would like to use an example from "Story 28: Majority". As I don't share all my hobbies with my husband, our aim when planning a holiday is to find a holiday destination where we can both do what we both enjoy.

What exactly is my goal – the process or the end result? Do I want to search or find, do or finish something, learn or master, wait or meet ("Story 1: Searching or finding...?")?

In the example with the neighbour, the formulation 'I am very satisfied with my comfortable flat and the pleasant relationships with my neighbours' is the end result, since that is exactly what I wanted to achieve.

What do I really want – certain events, things, acquaintances or positive feelings, and namely that these feelings are reflected in all aspects of my wish that are of interest to me ("Story 3: When dreams come true..." and "Story 19: Coincidences are never a coincidence...")?

The wording 'I am very satisfied with my comfortable flat and the pleasant relationships with my neighbours' expresses both positive feelings about the flat – "very satisfied", and about the relationships with the neighbours – "pleasant".

> *I also had wishes in which the wording did not contain pleasant feelings, for example: 'I would like to help the unemployed find work'. I did find such a job, but I didn't feel good about it ("Story 3: When dreams come true...").*

In my wishes, do I adhere to other people's beliefs and rules or to my own ("Story 11: When you try to please everybody")?

Do I really want the formulated wish to be fulfilled and am I prepared to take steps to achieve the goal ("Story 19: Coincidences are never a coincidence...")?

> *In the example with the neighbour, I was not only prepared to act, but also took all the possible steps that are described in detail in "Story 10: Making things worse for the better".*

> *There were other wishes, such as fasting, quitting smoking, looking younger or finding out which hairstyles and hair colours suit me. Although these wishes arose at different stages of my life, they were united by the fact that I had no particular willingness to take steps towards realising them. There was another thing that all these wishes had in common. Pleasant feelings were missing in their formulations, and they all came true during my hepatitis C treatment when I was not doing so well ("Story 19: Coincidences are never a coincidence...").*

I also take the following points into account:

If I don't know exactly what I want, but I do know what I want to feel, then, strangely enough, I find that too. As an example, I would like to cite a situation from "Story 8: I don't know what I want – I don't want what I know...":

> *I formulated the goal very vaguely because I didn't know which job I wanted to do, so I focussed on the feeling:*
>
> - *I am thrilled by what I do, and by where, how and with whom I do it*
> - *my customers, colleagues, employer and I are very satisfied with my performance*

Since my unconscious ignores negations such as "not", "un-" and "no", I use positive words when formulating my affirmations. In this case, I would like to mention an example from "Story 18: Endlessly positive!":

> *At the time, I was actively learning German and didn't want to be afraid of making and answering phone calls in German. As this formulation only*

made me even more afraid, I decided to reformulate the wish so that it made me feel good. This turned 'I'm not afraid' into 'I'm calm, understand what I'm being told and can formulate and explain my thoughts in German'.

In some cases, I ask myself whether I should wish for a specific outcome or whether it is better to aim for the best possible outcome. After all, how do I know if the good outcome is really the one that I consider to be good? I'll use an example from "Story 31: A conversation with the shadows":

In the past, I often wished for a certain outcome, for example from a job interview. My wish was something like this: 'I want to get a job at this institution'. Every time I got a rejection, I was disappointed. It was only after I had found a job with which I was very satisfied that I was happy to have received rejections from all the other institutions. Then I thought about whether it wouldn't be better to wish for something else, so as not to become unnecessarily frustrated. After some reflection, I came up with the following formulation: 'I want the interview to go as well as possible for me and for the other party'. If nothing materialised, I thought that it wasn't what I needed and reacted calmly to the outcome of the conversation.

Negative thoughts and desires lead to negative consequences. Here are some examples:

When I was young, the separation from the young man I loved was such a tragedy for me that I didn't want to go on living. A few months after our last encounter, I found myself in a situation from which I miraculously emerged alive and well ("Story 15: It is better to die and to be left in peace...").

Shortly before I was diagnosed with hepatitis C, I found myself in a difficult living situation from which I saw no way out. I went through various future scenarios in my head, but they all scared me. As a result, I found myself falling deeper and deeper into a negative spiral and was very afraid for the future ("Story 33: Peace and comfort!").

As soon as I have formulated an affirmation, I check it against the positive and negative checklists. Then, if necessary, I correct the wording and check it again.

Positive Checklist

*If at least one point from the list is **not ticked**, I will revise the wording of the affirmation.*

- ☐ The wording fills me with joy.
- ☐ All aspects of the desired outcome are formulated positively and in the present tense.
- ☐ The formulation contains the positive emotions of the desired result.
- ☐ My wish or goal is the end result.

Negative Checklist

*If at least one point from the list **is ticked**, I will revise the wording of the affirmation.*

- ☐ I don't feel comfortable with the wording.
- ☐ The desired outcome harms me or can have a negative impact on me.
- ☐ The wish or goal harms others.
- ☐ There is a negation such as "not", "un-" or "no" in combination with negative words in the formulation of the affirmation.

After reviewing the two checklists, and if everything is okay with the formulation, I add the affirmation to the "My happy life" list that I work with every day. This technique is explained in detail in "Chapter 5: Basic Practices", in the section "Working with affirmations".

When setting myself a new goal, I generally pay attention to my dreams because they sometimes show me the consequences of my intentions. There is more on this in "Chapter 5: Basic Practices", in the section "Working with dreams".

My wishes and goals are not set in stone, but can change over time. As I work with them, I sometimes adapt them – adding to them, making them more precise or reformulating them.

Exercise 4:

Check the wording of your wishes that you have written down in the lists "What am I grateful for in life?" and "What do I wish for in life?". Modify them as necessary and add the affirmations to the "My happy life" list ("Chapter 6: Your Gratitude and Manifestation Journal", in the section "My happy life").

Step 3:
Taking action

After adding a goal to the "My happy life" list, I move on to planning the steps to achieve this goal (Figure 5 "Step 3: Taking action").

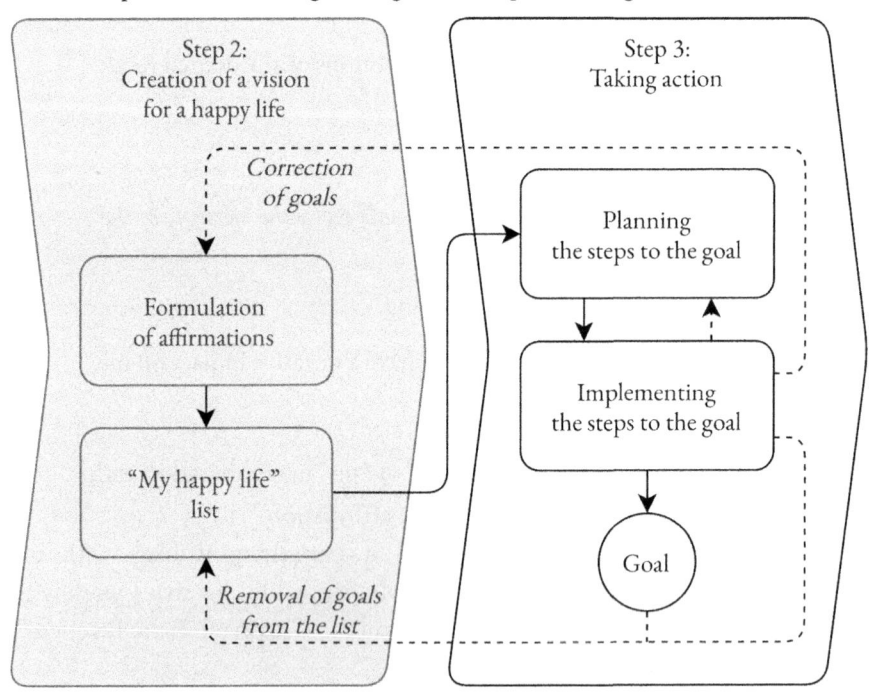

Figure 5 Step 3: Taking action

I start with the question of how soon I want to reach my goal. In some cases, this question is easy to answer but is very difficult in others.

> For example, when my husband found a new job in another city, we had to find an apartment by a certain date ("Story 8: I don't know what I want – I don't want what I know...").

> When I wanted to become an electrical engineer, I knew from the outset that it would take five and a half years to study at university.

> When I wanted to lead seminars for a particular organisation, I had no concrete idea of how long it would take to achieve my goal and whether it was even possible. However, after three and a half years, I reached my goal

> *("Story 7: God moves in mysterious ways")*.

If I have an idea of how long it will take to achieve the goal, I set it; if not, I don't. I proceed in the same way when planning steps. For each goal I set, I plan at least one step and start implementing it.

> *In the case of seminars, I could not imagine how I could achieve this goal but the first step was clear to me, and I initially began to lead such seminars in my mother tongue for another organization ("Story 7: God moves in mysterious ways")*.

If it is a goal arising from a problem, when planning the steps, I take into account the possibilities for achieving the goal that I saw when analysing the problem. Problem analysis is described in detail in "Chapter 5: Basic Practices", in the section "Working with problems".

When planning steps, I start with the question, 'What steps do I see towards the goal?'. Here is an example from "Story 8: I don't know what I want – I don't want what I know…":

> *The goal was rather vaguely formulated. The focus was more on feelings than on concrete things:*
>
> - *I am thrilled by what I do, and by where, how and with whom I do it*
> - *my customers, colleagues, employer and I are very satisfied with my performance*
>
> *Now I move on to answering the question:*
> *'What steps did I see towards my goal?'*
>
> - *draw up a list of all the institutions in the city that work with immigrants, since I have only dealt with foreigners so far*
> - *send unsolicited applications to various institutions and offer all the knowledge and experience I have. (I didn't mention any job title, since I didn't know exactly what I wanted to do).*
> - *prepare for a job interview, in the event that I am invited for one*
>
> *Incidentally, although I didn't set myself a time frame for achieving my goal, I found a job within a month.*

As soon as I decide on a step, I go to bed with the intention of implementing what I have planned, and in the morning, I then analyse the dreams that I had.

This technique is explained in detail in "Chapter 5: Basic Practices", in the section "Working with dreams". I repeat the same thing for each new step.

Sometimes I have ideas about my plans at night. I then write them down immediately because otherwise I won't be able to remember them in the morning.

After completing a step, I check whether the goal has been achieved and, if not, I ask myself whether the goal is still relevant. If it is, I plan the next step and the cycle repeats until I reach my goal.

If the situation changes, I either correct the goal or abandon it and remove it from the "My happy life" list.

Here is an example from "Story 2: A healthy dose of complacency":

During my studies, I had the opportunity to take part in a competition for a scholarship to train as a systemic counsellor.

My first step was to apply for the competition. After I was selected as a candidate for the scholarship, the goal had not yet been achieved but was still relevant to me.

In the next step, I submitted all the necessary documents to the institution that awarded the scholarships, but I received a rejection. As a result, the goal was not achieved and became irrelevant for me.

After giving up this goal, the situation changed again. To my great surprise, I received the scholarship.

Once I have achieved the goal, I ask myself whether or not I should keep it on the "My happy life" list. If I want what I have achieved to continue to bring me joy, for example my job, which I love, then I leave the goal on the list. If the goal is no longer relevant once it has been achieved, such as receiving a scholarship, I cross it off the list.

To achieve my goals, I pay attention to the following points:

If possible, I always keep my goals in mind, so that I don't get lost on the way ("Story 25: The finger points at the moon"). It also helps me to recognise opportunities for realising my intentions ("Story 7: God moves in mysterious ways").

If I want something I don't just think about it, I also take steps to achieve it – if it is within my control. Otherwise, life may force me to do it anyway ("Story 19: Coincidences are never a coincidence…").

I also realised that it is better not to wait for someone to make my wish come true, but to actively participate in the realisation of my wish ("Story 5: Share your smiles").

There are goals for which steps seem clear. There are also those for which there is no prescribed path. But if I really want something and move in the right direction, I will still somehow achieve the desired goal ("Story 7: God moves in mysterious ways").

If I am only clear about one step, I concentrate on realising it and always keep my goal in mind instead of trying to anticipate the next steps, as sometimes I can only see the next step when I have finished the current one. ("Story 25: The finger points at the moon").

The path to a goal can bring surprises that I am only able to understand once I have reached the goal. Not everything that I perceive as negative today will look negative to me tomorrow; the same goes for something positive. That's why I stay as relaxed as possible on the way to a goal ("Story 12: What is good and what is bad?").

On the way to a goal, there are always situations that initially appear to slow down or hinder the achievement of the goal. In moments like these, I ask myself, 'What opportunities does this offer me?' After all, if I had an opportunity and didn't take advantage of it, then it's as if I didn't have any at all ("Story 13: Take advantage of opportunities!").

It is often only when the last hope dies, and inner peace comes, that opportunities arise ("Story 15: It is better to die and to be left in peace...").

On the way to a goal, I prefer to rely on myself ("Story 22: The buck stops here!") and do my best despite feeling afraid ("Story 16: Fortune smiles on the brave!").

The best results can be achieved with love ("Story 20: Love can move mountains!").

I would also like to talk about intuition. I prefer to act on it immediately, otherwise I may be dissatisfied with the result ("Story 14: Listen to your intuition!").

Exercise 5:

Use a notebook for this exercise or create notes in digital format.

Learn to achieve goals under uncertain conditions.

For this exercise, choose a goal from the "My happy life" list ("Chapter 6: Your Gratitude and Manifestation Journal", in the section "My happy life"), for which you cannot imagine the entire path to the goal, and write it down.

By when do you want to achieve this goal?

If you have an idea of how long it will take to achieve the goal, specify it; if not, leave this question unanswered.

What steps do you see towards the goal?

Write them down. If it is a goal derived from a problem, look at the options for achieving the goal that you wrote down when analysing the problem.

Choose a step that you want to take first and concentrate on implementing it.

Have you achieved the goal?

If you have not yet achieved the goal, check whether the goal is still relevant to you.

If the goal is still relevant to you, select the next step and implement it. Repeat until you reach the goal.

CHAPTER 5:

BASIC PRACTICES

Working with problems

I usually prefer to solve problems as they arise. If there are a lot of problems, I start with what bothers me the most. When analysing a problem, I write down my thoughts on paper or digitally, as new ideas only come to me after I have written down the ideas that have been buzzing around in my head.

I pay particular attention to the following points:

As long as I saw the causes of my problems exclusively in external factors, I had the impression that I was a victim of circumstances and that nothing depended upon me. If anyone could solve the problem, I certainly wasn't the one to do it. Shifting the focus of my attention from the external circumstances to myself enabled me to realise that I was involved in creating these problems, and thereby discover new ways to solve them.

I also realised that unpleasant feelings are an indication that I am doing something wrong. If I change my behaviour, both the situation and my feelings change. Here is an example:

There was a time when I didn't feel comfortable in my relationship with my son. As long as I thought he had to change his behaviour in order to normalise it, nothing happened. It was only when I started to change my behaviour that our relationship became normal again ("Story 17: And just where is the happy medium...?").

One of the causes of relationship problems can be that I mainly focus on negative things and don't value the positive ones sufficiently.

What helped me to solve the problem in my relationship with my son was to restore a balance, i.e. I started to talk not only about what I didn't like, but also about all the positive things that I hadn't talked about before because I had taken them for granted ("Story 17: And just where is the happy medium...?").

There are a few other points that I pay attention to:

Sometimes I saw the cause of my problems in my convictions, negative thoughts, lack of attention to all important aspects when formulating my wishes, or lack of attention to what brings me joy. Here are some examples:

I would like to start with the problem that was caused by my convictions.

> *Ever since I was a child, I was taught that I had to do everything perfectly and so I developed a fear of making mistakes. It wasn't until many years later, as an adult, that I managed to overcome this fear ("Story 21: And then along came happiness").*

In the following example, I saw my negative thoughts as the cause of the problem:

> *When I was young, I broke up with the young man I loved. It was such a tragedy for me that I didn't want to go on living. A few months after our last encounter, I found myself in a situation from which I miraculously emerged alive and well ("Story 15: It is better to die and to be left in peace...").*

In the next example, I move on to the lack of attention to all important aspects when formulating my wishes:

> *In our previous house we lived next door to nice neighbours. I had got so used to it that, when I moved, I thought of many things I wanted in a new apartment: it had a balcony, was in the centre of a town I liked, there was plenty of parking nearby and I could walk to work in ten minutes. However, I forgot to think about good neighbours.*
>
> *After a while, we moved to a very nice spa town where my husband found a job. Our apartment had a balcony, the building was in the city centre, there was a large car park nearby and, when I found a job, I was surprised that it took me exactly ten minutes to walk to work. I actually got everything I wanted from our new apartment. There were also things I hadn't thought about, both positive (the garage) and negative (the neighbour, with whom, as it later turned out, other residents of our building also had problems – see "Story 10: Making things worse for the better").*

In this example, I come to the lack of attention for the things that gave me joy:

> *Everything I wanted from my new job was in place. Even my colleagues, with whom I really enjoyed working. I was very happy about it at first. Over time, I got used to it and stopped paying attention. Then I got a colleague with whom I didn't get on so well with ("Story 4: Can we all win...? Of course!").*

Let me summarise the above. For every problem:

- I shift the focus from external circumstances to myself
- I think about whether my beliefs are the cause of the problem
- I pay attention to the connection between my behaviour and my feelings in order to understand which of my actions lead to negative feelings
- I remember the thoughts and wishes that preceded the problem

Then I ask myself the following reflective questions for each problem:

- what brings discomfort into my life?
- what do I see as the cause of the problem?
- have I, or someone close to me, ever had a similar problem? And, if so, how did I, or this person, manage to overcome it?
- what options do I see for solving the problem?

As an example, I would like to take a closer look at the situation with my neighbour from "Story 10: Making things worse for the better".

What brought discomfort into my life?

The neighbour regularly made unfounded allegations against us, tried to turn the other neighbours against us and complained about us under false pretences to various authorities.

What did I see as the cause of the problem?

One aspect was missing when I formulated my wish, namely nice neighbours in the house. If my husband and I had prioritised this point, we would have at least asked the landlord and some neighbours if there were any problematic tenants in the house.

Have I, or someone close to me, ever had a similar problem? And, if so, how did I, or this person, manage to overcome it?

Many years ago, we had a troublesome neighbour. When we started to ignore him, he stopped bothering us.

There was a neighbour in my parents' house who was an alcoholic and wouldn't leave anyone alone. All the residents of the house signed a petition to the property management, demanding that they solve the problem, and soon the neighbour moved.

What options did I see to solve the problem?

I could:

- *make concessions to the neighbour*
- *complain to the property management about the neighbour*
- *find another apartment*
- *ignore the neighbour*
- *propose to the property management to ask the neighbours about who, among the tenants, is violating the house rules*

Exercise 6:

Use a notebook for this exercise or create notes in digital format.

Choose a problem that is currently bothering you.

Answer the following questions for this problem:

- what brings discomfort into my life?
- what do I see as the cause of the problem?
- have I, or someone close to me, ever had a similar problem? And, if so, how did I, or this person, manage to overcome it?
- what options do I see for solving the problem?

Working with affirmations

The main tool I work with every day is the "My happy life" list.

Every morning, upon waking up, I gratefully list all affirmations from this list. Finally, I give thanks that everything went well for me today. During the day, I concentrate on my daily activities. In the evening, before going to sleep, I start with gratitude for today and then go through my list of affirmations.

To prepare myself for this practice, I imagine a stream of love into which I immerse myself and dissolve.

Sometimes I also go through my list in my head during the moments of the day when I am relaxed and have positive feelings. For example, when listening to music, tidying the flat, travelling by bus, going for a walk, at the beach and so on ("Story 33: Peace and comfort!").

In addition, when I am overwhelmed by negative emotions, I also list my affirmations from the list.

I pay particular attention to my state of mind in relation to my wishes. When I have a very strong desire to receive something, it is usually associated with an acute feeling of lack for what I want and, at the same time, the hope that it will come in the future. I realised that my wishes were fulfilled when I stopped hoping and waiting for them. I have gained the impression that the opportunities for fulfilling my wishes arise primarily when I am in the state: 'If I receive this, it's great, if not – also good'. Sometimes the hope and expectation only disappeared when I found myself in a situation in which the fulfilment of my wish seemed impossible ("Story 2: A healthy "don't care" attitude"). As I often realised that my wishes didn't come true just when I wanted them so badly, I began to adjust to the fact that things would be ok if this wish wasn't fulfilled, even though I wanted to make it come true. In this way, I was able to transform hope into a healthy "don't care" attitude.

When it comes to visualising goals, I have an ambivalent attitude. On the one hand, it helps me to visualise what I want to achieve. On the other hand, it can also be a limitation. Here is an example:

My husband and I were living in a rented apartment and wanted to buy a property. We had a clear idea of the kind of property we wanted and which neighbourhoods would suit us best. We even found photos that exactly reflected our ideas about the property. We constantly monitored the property listings, viewed various properties, but found nothing that appealed to us.

> *At some point, we decided to focus our desire only on the feelings that the property and the neighbourhood would evoke in us, and no longer imagine the appearance and the specific location. What we found far exceeded what we could have imagined. Our imagination was clearly not powerful enough to visualise what we might enjoy ("Chapter 2: From Gratitude to Manifestation", in the section "A brief report 10 years later").*

Through these experiences, I came to the conclusion that focussing on feelings in my wishes can lead to results that exceed even my wildest expectations. That's why I use a tool such as visualisation very carefully.

When it comes to the lifestyle I want to achieve or what I like about my current life, I like to use visualisation. If I want something specific, as in the example with the property, I ask myself, 'Can the visualisation of what I want be a restriction?'. If so, I only concentrate on feelings.

Exercise 7:

You will find the affirmation and visualisation exercise in "Chapter 6: Your Gratitude and Manifestation Journal", in the sections "Affirm your happy life", "Visualise your happy life" and "Enjoy your day").

Working with feelings and emotions

I consider feelings to be a kind of barometer. Positive feelings show me what I like in my life. Negative feelings make me aware of what brings discomfort into my life and what I should change.

When I feel negative emotions rising up inside me, I mentally list my wishes and goals from my list until I calm down.

When something upsets me and my emotions boil up, I shift my attention away from the negative thoughts and instead focus on positive ones, so that the negative emotions reinforce the positive thoughts ("Story 30: Bless you!").

> *When some of my neighbour's actions triggered strong negative emotions in me, along with negative thoughts, I immediately remembered my wish and repeated it until I calmed down: 'I am very satisfied with my comfortable flat and pleasant relationships with my neighbours' ("Story 10: Making things worse for the better").*

In moments in which I am overwhelmed by strong emotions, I also use positive words and include negation, for example instead of "sick" I say "not healthy", instead of "sad" – "not happy" etc., so that my subconscious serves my best interests ("Story 18: Endlessly positive!").

If something that often occurs in my life causes me anxiety, for example an activity, I start to do it regularly. This results in the fear disappearing. And the sooner I start doing it and the more often I do it, the faster this happens.

> *When I was teaching, it was the exact opposite. For years, I even avoided teaching because my fear of public speaking haunted me all the time. At some point, I decided to get over it. After completing further courses as a trainer in adult education, I started to lead seminars. Over time, the fear became less and less until it finally disappeared completely ("Story 9: It makes me afraid...? Try it!").*

There are other types of fear, for example the fear of not conforming to an ideal that was propagated by my upbringing or invented by myself. If I allow myself to be less than perfect, the reason for the fear disappears.

> *The perfectionism I had internalised since childhood was, on the one hand, an incentive to improve my skills but, on the other, the cause of all manner of fears: making a mistake, appearing incompetent, etc.*

> *While attending various training courses, I paid attention to teachers who spoke openly about not knowing something or not being able to answer a question immediately. Such moments were met with understanding by course participants, which gave me the courage to behave in a similar way. As soon as I allowed myself to be less than perfect, the fears disappeared ("Story 21: And then along came happiness").*

When I am afraid of the future, I shift my focus from fear of the unknown to my wishes.

> *Every time I was afraid of the thought of having to lead seminars the following year without my colleague, with whom I had really enjoyed working, I would say to myself, 'I am very glad that everything went well for both me and my colleague'. I kept repeating this sentence until I calmed down and shielded myself from negative thoughts ("Story 23: Over and over again...").*

Exercise 8:

Learn to make negative emotions work positively for you.

Choose a short positive phrase that makes you feel good. For example, it could be an affirmation from the "My happy life" list ("Chapter 6: Your Gratitude and Manifestation Journal", in the section "My happy life").

Every time you experience negative emotions, repeat this phrase until you calm down.

Exercise 9:

Learn to shift your attention from negative thoughts to the opposite.

Every time negative thoughts arise from an existing problem and cause negative feelings, repeat the affirmation from the "My happy life" list ("Chapter 6: Your Gratitude and Manifestation Journal", in the section "My happy life") that you have formulated in relation to this problem, until you calm down.

Working with dreams

When observing my dreams, I came to the conclusion that they often show me what consequences my actions or inaction can result in. In this way, they help me to recognise unresolved problems, as well as to correct my wishes, goals, steps towards the goal and current plans.

When I started to listen to the messages in my dreams, I gained confidence in my actions and an inner peace that I previously lacked. I would like to point out here that the longer I observe my dreams, the better I understand them.

I start with dreams that point to unresolved problems. For example, these can be recurring painful dreams with similar content and involving the same people ("Story 32: Are you in harmony with yourself...?"). I pay attention to how I behave in such dreams. Analysing my dreams allows me to identify my behaviour that leads to painful feelings in real life. When I start to behave differently, the feelings change both in the dream and in reality. When I decide to change my behaviour, I go to bed with the firm intention of doing so. The same goes for my current plans.

I put something to write with next to the bed (a notebook with a pen or a smartphone) so that I can make brief notes about my dreams at night, if necessary. They help me to remember my dreams in the morning.

If I haven't had any unpleasant dreams or no dreams at all, or if I can't remember my dreams, then I assume that everything is fine with my planned action.

If I don't feel comfortable with what I saw in the dream or have unpleasant feelings about the dream after waking up, then I either give up what I was planning to do or I change my intentions.

In my dreams, I can be myself or someone else. Other people do not necessarily have to represent themselves either. Only after waking up, do I have associations as to who was who in my dreams.

Sometimes my dream shows me the consequences of another person's intentions and not my own. If the consequences of another person's or group of people's behaviour cause me unpleasant feelings in the dream, I ask myself after waking up whether I can do anything to change the real-life situation from what it was in the dream. On the occasions when I have managed to change the situation in real life, the consequences have also been very different. Here is an example:

In the dream in which my husband was travelling alone in a defective car, the journey ended in disaster. In reality, I changed the situation by travelling with him, which led to a different outcome ("Story 32: Are you in harmony with yourself...?").

In some situations, I keep a dream diary. In the morning, I write down:

- the intention with which I went to bed
- what dreams I had

When describing a dream, I pay particular attention to the consequences of the actions – or failure to act – of the people in the dream, and to the feelings they evoked. I take the dream about my husband as an example:

What was my intention when I went to bed?

In this case, it was my husband's intention to drive the car.

What did I dream?

My husband drove the defective car alone. His classmates came to our house and told me that my husband would not be coming home. I screamed in fear and woke up.

I then think about what associations the events in the dream evoke in relation to my intentions.

In this case, I immediately thought of my husband, who wanted to drive a defective car.

When I have negative feelings in a dream, I ask myself one question: 'What can I change in reality so that the situation would be different than in the dream?'

In this case, I saw two options:

- *to persuade my husband to stay at home, but that didn't work*
- *to go with him*

It was similar with the recurring dreams that had caused me the same pain for many years. As soon as I changed my behaviour in reality, my dreams began to change and with them my feelings. Here is another example from "Story 32: Are you in harmony with yourself...?".

There was another person present in these dreams. We didn't speak to each other in real life for many years and we were also silent in our dreams. When I started communicating with him, I realised that we also started talking in our dreams. My feelings also changed, both in my dreams and in reality.

Thanks to the dream analysis technique described above, I was able to both clarify my relationship with this person and also get rid of the painful dreams.

Exercise 10:

Use a notebook for this exercise or create notes in digital format.

Before you use your dreams to plan steps, observe your dreams over a long period of time. Start keeping a dream journal.

Only analyse dreams that evoke positive or negative emotions within you.

Every day, make a plan for the next day and go to bed in the evening with the intention of implementing what you have planned.

Put something to write with next to your bed (a notebook with a pen or a smartphone) so that you can make short notes about your dreams at night, as necessary.

If you can remember your dream in the morning, describe it. When describing the dream, pay particular attention to the consequences of the actions or inactions of the people in the dream and the feelings they evoked.

Think about what associations the events in the dream evoke in relation to your intentions.

In the evening, make a note of the connections you noticed between your dream and the events of the day.

CHAPTER 6:

YOUR GRATITUDE AND MANIFESTATION JOURNAL

Do the exercises in this chapter while reading the second part of the book "Roadmap to Happiness". There you will find references to exercises as well as explanations and examples.

What am I grateful for in life?

Write down everything you are grateful for: what you like in your life and would also like to keep in the future.

What do I wish for in life?

Write down everything you want to achieve in your life.

My happy life

When you have finished the lists "What am I grateful for in life?" and "What do I wish for in life?" check the wording of your wishes and goals, adjust them as necessary and write them down here. You can either create one list or divide the list into topics such as health, family, relationships, career, finances, etc.

Affirm your happy life

Do this exercise every day when you wake up and before you go to sleep.

Close your eyes, relax, fill yourself with pleasant feelings, e.g. think of something that brings you joy, or imagine a stream of love into which you immerse yourself and dissolve.

Gratefully list all the affirmations on your list and visualise what you desire, as if your wish has already come true.

You can also make a sound recording, e.g. with your smartphone, and listen to your list.

Finish the morning by giving thanks that everything went well for you today. In the evening, start with gratitude for the day.

Visualise your happy life

Choose photos, pictures, drawings or objects that reflect the lifestyle you aspire to. Place them somewhere that you can see them every day.

Enjoy your day

During the day, focus your attention on your current activities.

As soon as you see an opportunity to achieve what you want, take action.

During the day, pay attention to the things that bring you joy.

Report on your progress

At a later date, report on the extent to which your wishes and goals have been fulfilled over the coming years.

1 year later

2 years later

3 years later

4 years later

5 years later

6 years later

7 years later

8 years later

9 years later

10 years later

ABOUT THE AUTHOR

Inna Turchyn was born in Ukraine in 1966. In 2002, at the age of 36, she emigrated with her family to Germany, where she worked as a counsellor in the field of immigrant integration, as a teacher of German as a second language, as a coach and trainer for career planning, and as a systemic counsellor for families with troubled children.

Even at a young age, she was interested in the question: 'What is the meaning of life?' To find an answer to this question, she read religious, philosophical, spiritual and esoteric literature, practised various techniques, such as positive thinking, meditation, visualisations, affirmations, and studied various areas of psychology.

One day she saw the meaning of life in being happy but, having been brought up to sacrifice her own well-being for the well-being of others, she didn't know how to achieve this goal.

Only after analysing her life in detail, during her hepatitis C therapy, did she become convinced that she could achieve this goal. By applying her approach, which she discovered in the course of her therapy, she not only managed to overcome a seemingly hopeless situation, but also to build a happy life.

Printed in Great Britain
by Amazon